Times of Mourning

Times of Mourning

Bereavement, Clinical Challenge, and Subjectivity

Adriana Bauab

Translated by Gabriel Sarmiento

Foreword by Isidoro Vegh

LEXINGTON BOOKS
Lanham • Boulder • New York • London

Published by Lexington Books
An imprint of The Rowman & Littlefield Publishing Group, Inc.
4501 Forbes Boulevard, Suite 200, Lanham, Maryland 20706
www.rowman.com

6 Tinworth Street, London SE11 5AL, United Kingdom

British Library Cataloguing in Publication Information Available

Library of Congress Cataloging-in-Publication Data on File

ISBN: 978-1-7936-1775-0 (cloth)
ISBN: 978-1-7936-1776-7 (electronic)

Contents

Foreword

Psychoanalysis addressed the issue of mourning from an early time. Its creator, Sigmund Freud, questioned its causes from the beginning of his practice. It's that his patients brought to him the halted, encrusted pain of their losses that was manifested in their symptoms, their inhibitions.

This book, which recognizes its predecessors in the Freudian clinic, moves forward with the new life that Lacan's teachings contributed to psychoanalysis. References to his seminars and writings are made throughout the book in what is a thoughtful and stimulating read.

This led the author to her own formulations, which today she offers to us in a generous display:

1) In the times of mourning.
2) In a renewed metapsychology with reflections on the termed object which is relayed to the *jouissance* of drive and, by its lack, to desire.
3) To its relation to the successes and failures of sexuation and the validity, or invalidity, of the Names-of-the-Father.
4) Its incidences in the body and the commonly named physical pathologies: hysteria, hypochondria, psychosomatic phenomena.
5) Clinical accounts that situate the "limit of the structure" as the paradigmatic finale of Walter Benjamin.
6) The interventions which that clinical practice suggests for the efficacy of the treatment.
7) The incidences in the culture and polis of rejected or assumed mourning.

Its enunciation exhibits in action the mourning of an all-knowing one in the questions made explicit or suggested for each topic undertaken. This is also seen in the inviting texts of other authors which introduce a creative twist.

Thus the quote from Safouan that maintains that "every mourning is about encountering a truth, though that truth isn't always necessarily the same. But it's a truth that always concerns the structure more than the person or the psyche."

Which carries the author to the conclusion: "We understand, then, that the work of mourning is the occasion to access a certain knowledge about the limits of the structure, about the moment when the object was constituted."

An invitation to the reader: this book does not claim to be equal to the Ideal. It offers itself as an opportunity for a critical, creative exercise.

Isidoro Vegh
January 2001

Introduction

The term "mourning" is the translation for the Spanish word *duelo*, and *duelo* is a homonym with two meanings that befall it. Etymologically, it comes from two Latin words[1]:

- The Late Latin term *Dolus*, which means pain, sorrow, or affliction. They are gestures that are made to manifest the feelings that one has because of someone's death.
- *Duellum*, an archaic phonetic variant of *bellum*, which means battle, challenge, combat between two.

The prior references describe the definition of mourning given its current use in our language. Nonetheless, Sigmund Freud, in his renowned essay *Mourning and Melancholia*, stamped the term "mourning" with psychoanalytical roots. That is, starting with that text from 1915, the anemic state and the vicissitudes that are brought about because of mourning, with respect to processing the loss, are subjects of great interest for psychoanalysis. Therein the affection of mourning is associated, contrasted with, and differentiated from one of the most controversial entities in the field of the psyche, melancholy.

Said essay starts off like so

> dreams having served us as the prototype in normal life of narcissistic mental disorders, [he had just finished reflecting on the structural difference between psychotic hallucination and the constitution of dreamlike images in *A Metapsychological Supplement to the Theory of Dreams*] we will now try to throw some light on the nature of melancholia by comparing it with the normal affect of mourning.[2] (Freud 1957a, 243)

Basing ourselves on the homonymous property of the word *duelo* (mourning), and of the previously mentioned etymological roots, we can affirm that mourning is pain, a psychic pain which can even come to affect the body, as is the case with some psychosomatic disorders. But it's also a challenge for the subjective structure to reconstruct its symbolic universe after the shockwave that caused the hole in the real which means the loss of the loved object.

Mourning is a concept where the way that a community or collective structure tackles the subject of death—through rituals and ceremonies displayed within the cultural and religious heritage—and the unquestionably personal dimension that its phenomena express in the singularity of each case come together.

This characteristic of the topic is made evident in the fact that *Mourning and Melancholia* was a contemporary of—in the year 1915—another article called *Thoughts for the Times on War and Death*, with its denomination as being for the times, contains an essay that touches on the subject of man's attitude toward death.

The current topic at the time was World War I. It had been just a few months since it had kicked off, and it appears that it had given Freud the impetus to initiate deep reflections on the topic of death. Wrapped in the whirlwind of that time of war—where weapons were developing at an unprecedented speed up to that time—man changed substantially with its attitude toward death.

In times of war, this didn't just come about naturally, accidentally, or on occasion. It was no longer the death of medieval poetry, which had so poetically described the saga of Spanish lyrical epics of the Romanceros of the fifteenth and sixteenth centuries.[3] Here death announced its proximity, and despite the Reaper bringing about despair and pleas for its absence throughout all ages, in those times it was received without a big fuss, sometimes even received complacently. With a war being unleashed of such magnitude as was the Great War, it is man who goes and meets his probable death at the battle front, where it's massified and depersonalized.

As Freud says in *Thoughts for the Times on War and Death*, war produces a substantial transformation in the attitude of man toward death. They no longer allow themselves to deny it; it's necessary to believe in it. Men don't die one by one, but a multitude at once, in just one day.

In his book *The Hour of Our Death*, Philippe Aries wrote:

> In the early twentieth century, before World War I, throughout the Western world of Latin culture, be it Catholic or Protestant, the death of a man still solemnly altered the space and time of a social group that could be extended to include the entire community. The shutters were closed in the bedroom of the dying man, candles were lit, holy water was sprinkled; the house was filled with

> grave and whispering neighbors, relatives and friends . . . a notice of bereavement was posted on the door. (Aries 2008, 559)

Making a clear distinction between current times and those of that age, he commented,

> In the course of the twentieth century an absolutely new type of dying has made an appearance in some of the most industrialized, urbanized and technologically advanced areas of the Western world. . . . Society no longer observes a pause; the disappearance of an individual no longer affects its continuity. Everything in town goes on as if nobody died anymore. (Aries 2008, 560)

Jacques Lacan, on his part, repeatedly emphasized that the work of mourning is carried out on the level of logos, identifying this with the group or community. These, organized culturally, are their supports. He sustains the importance of supportive funeral rites and ceremonies in the work of mourning.

Taking up again Freud's question about what the work of mourning consists in, he proposes that it's, in the first place, a satisfaction, an impulsive requirement, in the function of the structural insufficiency of signifying elements to face the hole created in existence—in the real—which every loss entails.

As we were saying, there is a close relationship between mourning, the work of mourning processed in the singularity of each case, and the subjectivity of the era. There is an area of intersection between them. Faced with the real and irremediability of death, that which doesn't register in the unconscious, the whole signifying system mobilizes; the symbolic order is disturbed. The absence, a paradigm of castration while the support of the neurotic structure loses its location, staggers the phantasmatic equilibrium, and the subject is sent again to a place of deprivation. Faced with the loss of that object of love that acted as a cause, a subjective upheaval occurs, and it's typical that a series of clinical phenomena linked to different illnesses emerge. We propose that at the level of the subjective structure, said phenomena are the exhibitions of the suspension of castration as an operating function, and it's replacement for a more precarious mechanism for subjectivity: deprivation.

As Lacan described in detail in Seminar IV, *The Object Relation* (1956–1957), there are three logical operations of subjective constitution with respect to the object and the agent which carries it out: frustration, deprivation, and castration. They are operations that define modes of subjective orientation with respect to the status of the lack as imaginary in the first, real in the second, and symbolic in the third. When we say that during bereavement the subject is sent again to a position of deprivation, we refer to a movement which we understand in the following manner: a real loss of a symbolic object, since it acts as a lack in the structure, responds to a logic of incompleteness, affects the subject, and the agent which caused it—in the desperate search to place the blame of the loss on someone—is purely imaginary. That's why the subject frequently blames themselves, more or less consciously, for having been responsible for the loss that they endured. The feeling of guilt is common with those that martyr themselves. It's a corrosive feeling of guilt that is a maximum imagined expression of the devastating enjoyment (*jouissance*) of the Other.

From this place of deprivation, and faced with the impossibility of representation in the signifying chain, the subject appears. We say that they appear in the phenomena that are produced—inhibitory, addictive, hallucinatory, dietary, compulsive—a vassalage of the superego that sentence the subject to sacrifices and immolation. They are phenomena that, on occasion, will require analytical work so that they can acquire the status of symptoms.

Nonetheless, bereavements aren't only a breeding ground for illnesses, they can also be a chance, an exquisite opportunity, so that the aforementioned signifying recomposition that the elaboration of the loss entails constitute the fertile area to subjectivize it, namely, to elevate it to the category of missing, and consequently foster a redistribution of *jouissance*. In other words, going through the periods of the elaboration of mourning brings with it the most complete fulfillment. This translates not only to the substitution of the object by another, but also to the transformation of the relationship of the subject with the phantasmatic object. It's an enabling operation that allows the acts to become prosperous in the tracks of desire, remaining intimately connected to an end in the field of sublimation.

Along that stretch, the function of mourning would consist in subjectivizing the loss, the place where the object is irreplaceable because it's encased in the condition of unique. Advancing in the work of mourning would entail, then, supplementing it with a new route, detecting a new, creative and subjective style of trait where the object's shine no longer dazzles, nor the weight of its shadow crushes. That real border that the letter of mourning provides permits the subject to circumscribe the loss and register it as absent. It's the way of identifying the heritage that the loss made present and transform it into a legacy.

The work of mourning becomes, then, a challenge to produce that signifying recomposition that permits them to make the instituting lack available, recreating it. I'd like to highlight, then, that shift between what find in Freud to be the *work of mourning*, and what in Lacan we find as *function of mourning*.

We propose that the *function of mourning*, if its elaboration involves a function, is subjectivating. It applies to change in the subjective position, a reorganization of the libidinal load with respect to phantasmatic object, a transformation of the distribution of *jouissance*.

Whether it be a normal reaction, or as work, mourning can stumble over difficulties, avatars in the logical periods of its procession. In clinical work, the manifestations of pathological mourning are diverse. They can present themselves as melancholy, that is, with the phenomenology of mourning that makes their mood be sad and the generalized inhibition of the ego, but extending indefinitely and immutably in time and being characterized by not having a register of the object, whose loss installed the anemic sorrow.

Likewise, they can manifest themselves in the modality of repetitive acting out, those subjects that go through life committing acts that are detached from their desire, deviating from who they are, committing permanent misunderstandings as if they were in a comedy of errors. We could assert, then, that in these cases the *out* in acting out is *out of the subjective position.*

On occasion the expression of a bereavement whose elaboration is exceedingly hampered or rejected propels the subject to a *passage à l'acte* which casts them *out of the worldly stage.*

Addictions to food, as is the case with bulimia, or not eating anything, as with anorexia, alcohol, drugs, or psychoactive drugs frequently begin with a significant loss.

Psychosomatic phenomena have also been found to be triggered by a rupture with the loved object. This doesn't only come as a shadow that falls over them and split the ego, but also to be embodied in the real fabric of the body.

All of these manifestations are expressions of the drive untied from the gorges of the signifier, adjusting the mode of expression, of instinctual satisfaction, which is distinguished from neurotic symptoms. Let's recall the definition of symptom as the formation of engagement stemming from a struggle between psychical instances, in which desire is overshadowed, and the subject is represented by the illness. In these cases, what's important isn't the symptomatic representation, but what is exhibited. The illness doesn't have the formal casing of a symptom, but it presents itself unwrapped, you might say, as a phenomenon.

Keeping up with Freud and Lacan's detours on the subject, it's laid down that there are periods of elaboration, of subjective orientation in the face of the loss, which are periods that in the clinical study which concerns us are identifiable, yet not obvious. They can't be skipped or spared. Losses, whether they're temporary or, even more so if they're irreparable, are unavoidable circumstances over the course of life. Some losses demand and require something to be done with them. They require some time to allow for crossing that dimension where the hole in existence is, and to install there the place where the subject can recognize and symbolize the structural lack. It's the structural lack that remits the lack in being in the subject, and its reciprocal, the castration of the Other.

That's why for each particular case, the term "mourning" can come to have different connotations. As far as the most intimate aspect, it can be thought of with respect to some loss, and how it determined a before and after in their lives, and how they went through the different periods of libidinal detachment from the loved object, reinvestment and redistribution of the libidinal load in Freudian terms. After this structural setback, the function of mourning, if it operates, fosters the restoration of links and resumptions for the subject. It's a function of mourning that reinscribes the place destined for the object while lacking and reinstates the order of desire.

NOTES

1. Translator's note: the Spanish word for mourning is *duelo*, which is a homonym. It can mean mourning or duel, as shown in the second bullet point.

2. José Etcheverry, the Spanish translator of Freud's works, points out that the German term *trauer*, just like the English *mourning* and Spanish *duelo*, can mean both the painful feeling and its outward manifestation.

3. To name one, let's remember the well-known romance of the "Enamorado y la Muerte" (The Man in Love and Death): "I was dreaming a dream last night, a dream of my soul, I was dreaming about my loves and that I was holding them in my arms / I saw a lady come in, so white / whiter than the driven snow. / Where did you get in, my love? / How did you get in, my love? The doors are closed and so are the windows and shutters. / I am not love, my lover, but Death sent to you by God. / O cruel death, let me live one more day! / You may not have a day, just one more hour of life." Translated by Gabriel Sarmiento.

Chapter 1

Mourning

A Psychoanalytical Concept

THE TIMES OF MOURNING

We'll start with a classic: *Mourning and Melancholia*. I think it best to note that Freud's big question that pierces the whole text could be formulated in the following manner: Why is it, given identical influences, tied to the loss of something loved, that what makes a hole in the real results in melancholy in many subjects instead of mourning?

Freud responds by posing the possibility of a pathological disposition present in these people that exhibit melancholy. What is this pathological disposition? We have advanced a few steps with Freud and Lacan to detach ourselves from the weight of phylogenetics being the determinant in the structure. That disposition to fall ill or not can be read in the light of the operational framework conceived by the *parlêtre*, the speaking-being. It's about a subject brought forth in the functions of alienation and separation with respect to the Other, the place of the universe of signifiers. The disposition which we speak of, we understand as a disposition to the lack of and failure of inscription. A disposition that speaks of the position of the subject with respect to the lack of institution, of the available resources to draw on, of running through it, re-enunciating it, and deploying it.

Freud says, "Mourning is regularly the reaction to the loss of a loved person, or to the loss of some abstraction which has taken the place of one, such as one's country, liberty, an ideal, and so on" (Freud 1957a, 243). That hole in the real mobilizes the whole symbolic order. It creates shockwaves where if what's lacking is castration support, one loses its place, and the subject is dispatched to a place of deprivation from where their pain is manifested more as staging than the path of discursive articulation. In the clinical picture, this presents itself in that display, more on the side of the phenomenon than the symptom. "Phenomenon" is a term taken from Late Latin (*phaenormnon*) that itself came from Greek and meant "thing that appears." The phenomenon, unlike the symptom, firstly is disclosed, it shows itself outside of the structure, and as such is not the result of any structuring operation.

Among them we mention: phenomena of acting out, melancholy, anorexia and bulimia, psychosomatic phenomena, addictive phenomena, elementary phenomena as is the case in hallucinations.

Mourning and Melancholia is a work that tries to tackle the structural difference between a normal affection, which is to mourn because of the loss of something loved, and a psychopathological entity—or pathological disposition as Freud calls it—which is melancholy, whose origin and description trace back to antiquity, to the pre-Hippocratic era, and that later Aristotle, in his treatise named *Problema XXX.I*, described in detail.[1]

We were wondering what disposition it's about; what other name could we give to that pathological disposition. We propose then that in the economy of subjectivity, it's about the capacity that the subject has to deal with the loss. To deal with it in the sense of resorting to the symbolic and imaginary resources to stabilize the structure before the assault of the real, I say *the real* as that which generates the shockwaves. With Freud *trauma*, the unassimilable, is one of his versions that demands too much work bonding, linking, as long as it resists symbolization.

There are two modes of presentation which appertain to the real—that never cease to not be written about—which are impossible to register: sex and death. Concerning these, nothing can be anticipated. In this regard, the subject doesn't have *a priori* knowledge—there is always some level of knowledge, it's unarmed, helpless. Faced with the death of a loved one, or some significant loss to one's sexual body, one is defenseless. They are stumbling blocks to the real in which the whole symbolic order is moved, disordered. In reality, there are multiple objects that surround the subject, but only some losses cause a *hole in the real.* The real is what touches the inner core of the subject, one's essence. That which reaches the nerve point, the core of the body.

We said that this hole in the real disorders the symbolic order. If castration is the founding operation and the maximum expression of loss, the hole which provokes the real loss sends the subject to a place of deprivation. From that place one remains deprived of localizing one's loss, delimiting it, naming it, tracing its outlines in relation to the object. A range of observable clinical phenomena (some authors cluster them together in the clinical study known as borderline personality disorder because of its supposed divergence from neurosis) reveal such a breakdown of the structure.

With Freud we caution, since the first records of conversion hysteria, that clinical studies indicate that the *impasses*, what resists the processing of mournings, show up in the most diverse ways. Said Freudian records about hysteria combined for its manifestation not only the contact with sexual trauma, but also often times the loss of a loved one. At the roots of hysterical conversion, trauma as something sexual as well as trauma from a death converged, which triggered the symptoms of conversion disorder. Symptoms that appeared to be pervious to the effects of speech. In the most intimate depths of the discovery of the unconscious nests that peculiar way where the word spoken as interpretation alters the reality of the symptom.

Nonetheless, the practice that encouraged Freud appeared to dictate that under certain circumstances, the phenomena that these produce would not have a formal envelope[2] of the symptom as a formation of the unconscious. This would be purely about a phenomenon that appears unwrapped, manifesting thus the lack of proper formalization of a symptom in the psychoanalytic meaning of the term. We suggest that is how impeded mourning appears, stuck in its elaboration; pathological mourning which could be classified as *melancholized mourning.*[3]

That is why we understand, in the classic text from 1915, that Freud proposes a development work for mourning that entails having logical periods of completion. From the first moment, where what holds sway is the mechanism of disavowal or denial, until a posthumous moment where, after victimizing the object, provoking for a second time its loss, the libido would remain available for investment in other objects.

Returning to what we propose as the title of the present work, we'll say that going through a mourning process requires a multiplicity of periods, not only because it falls upon chronological development but also because it concerns a logic where different periods of subjective positioning are distinguishable.

This is how we describe the *first period*: faced with a real loss, the first response is to refuse to accept it, denial—*Verleugnung*—dispatches the subject to a deprived state, and from there, without recourse to remain represented in the signifying chain, it comes onto the stage. I understand that Freud places at the limit of this manifestation an entity that borders on psychosis, but isn't psychosis, the amentia of Meynert, or hallucinatory psychosis of desire.[4] The elementary phenomena of the hallucination present itself as an escape to retain the object; the price is losing touch with reality.

We could say then that to be in mourning, firstly it's about locating the absence, naming it, and accepting that something has been lost, not denying it. We already know about the essential role of funeral rites, of burials, in all civilizations as a way of confirming and registering the death of a loved one by the bereaved.

Freud, regarding the knowledge or lack of knowledge of the loss of something loved, proposed that there are different types of melancholy. Sometimes, he said, it's death that took away the loved one. Other times, it's the ups and downs of one's love life, disappointments that the subject suffers on occasion. The example that he used was that of a jilted lover.

Nevertheless, and paraphrasing Freud, it isn't just about knowing *who* was lost, but also *what* was lost along with the person who was lost. In this conjecture, we find the underlying notion that in order for the process of mourning to proceed and not get stuck in melancholy, it doesn't matter what was lost that causes the hole in the real for the subject. What's essential is if within the structure one operated within the established times of a particular mourning: that structure which the object constituted. Some subjects faced with any loss that implies the subtraction of a romantic relationship can't go through the process of mourning and succumb to melancholy. I stress the love of the mourning relationship with the narcissistic election of the object. On the world stage, facing the look of others, a subject can lose different objects. However, only a few will elicit mourning. We can establish those that have a narcissistic privilege.

The *second period* is strictly comprised of a symbolization process that implicates a large expenditure of energy, of inauguration, and of time. It's implemented piece by piece, and it carries with it a painful displeasure. This movement allows the subject to accept the reality that the loved object libidinally invested in is no longer there. It's the reality testing that makes it possible for the libido to withdraw its adherence to the object, now that there is no nuance, whether perceptive or sensory, that corresponds to the desire. Getting bogged down during this period of mourning, with stumbling blocks to advance and get through it, is what often makes bereavement become pathological, and what encases characteristics of melancholy.

Pathological comes from the Greek root *pathos*, which became a word to be used in the formation of words that indicate ailments or illnesses. It's a term that the Romans translated as *passio*, and which came to our language as passion. If we start with a characterization from the dictionary, *pathos* is what happens to someone or something, what is felt; it's not necessarily an experience of pain or suffering.[5] That is to say that the same ancient root word *pathos* derives a vocabulary that defines sickness on one side, and the passion, as in excitement and outbursts, that affects the subject on the other. We can suppose that it's at this same junction where bereavement becomes "pathological," that its most fruitful dimension and subjective stake can take root.

Sticking to the etymology, we could say that rooted in what's "pathological" in mourning links the possibility for a subject to undertake—on the path of subjectivizing the loss—an encounter with the loss, in a way that affects the subject without crushing them. On occasion, it's the operation of mourning itself that fosters and begins the search and encounter with deferred desires, or those desires with which one becomes passionate;

activities that can be linked to the field of sublimation, such as art, literature, or science.

What turns a normal reaction to a loss into pathological, demanding a clinical distinction between it and an entity such as melancholy?

From a phenomenological presentation, it's not immediately evident that there is a distinction—that's why it seems appropriate to us to base ourselves on the structural disposition with regards to the established loss. This will be an indicator that will divide the waters between mourning, that through its elaboration derives a normal reaction, or allows to draw out from one's *pathos*, that is one's own because of the pain involved, a stroke of creation, inspiration, and resumption from that other mourning, which due to being about a melancholic structure, has that path exceedingly hindered.

When it comes to melancholy, this path seems to be closed because the subject finds themselves immersed in the lack of knowledge of *what* was lost at the foundational moments, moments where the object is begotten.

In Freud's *Draft G* (1895), we read that on occasion melancholy is mourning; a mourning for the loss of libido. With melancholy it's about a libido that is not available because it did not serve the loss of Other, auguring an operational libidinal reserve[6] for the subject. We could say that there is a libidinal reserve that is brought about in foundational moments, and that the subject, today, hence doesn't have it available to affront the mourning process.

It's what Lacan redefines proposing:

> The problem of mourning is the problem of maintaining, at the scopic level, the bonds whereby desire is suspended, not from the object a, but from i(a), by which all love is narcissistically structured in so far as the term love implies the idealized dimension I spoke about. (Lacan 2014, 335)[7]

Maintaining the i(*a*),[8] the mirror image that is libidinized, when faced with mourning will depend on the operational libidinal reserve that the subjective warp can count on. A libidinal reserve is directly proportional to the subtraction of the (φ), imaginary phallus, in the foundational moments of the structure.

Thus, melancholy, or at times melancholized mourning, in that desperate attempt to separate from the overwhelming weight of the object, can produce the only effective act toward such purposes—suicide. It's the triumph of the object when it wasn't considered lost. This would be the opposite of what Freud proposes precisely to culminate the mourning process—and what I place as the *third period*—where the subject in an active position can effectuate for a second time the loss. Murdering the object, killing the dead person, or, in other words, losing in the symbolic what was lost in the real.

This movement allows for the modification of the ties to the lost object, the separation and the libidinal cathexis of other objects substituting the absence.

This is what we find in the classic text *Mourning and Melancholia*. Though we find the clarification in the last paragraph, as in so many of his other writings, the author considers his claims unfinished.

MOURNING AND *VERLEUGNUNG*

Disavowal, denial, and repudiation have been some ways of trying to translate into English the German term *Verleugnung*, used by Freud in different articles with meanings that weren't always consistent. While it first characterizes the prototypical mechanism of the perverse structure, near the end of the work it's presented as the essential process, a tributary of the *Spaltung* or splitting that slices through the subject.

As mentioned in *Some Psychical Consequences of the Anatomical Distinction between the Sexes* (1925) and later in *Fetishism* (1927), disavowal is the process by which the boy refuses to accept the mother's lack of a phallus, and as an adult, the mechanism where, via a fetish, it will allow him to keep the incompleteness of the Other veiled. Following the Freudian writing, we caution that that not wanting to know the difference between the sexes brings with it a withdrawal from a fragment of reality. Thus, we consider that the term *Verleugnung* was used to refer to the position of the subject with respect to reality, when this reality turns out to be intolerable for the self. Disavowing to accept the difference between the sexes, a patch of reality is also rejected. It's not about scotomization; it doesn't fall into the blind spot of their vision. On the contrary, it's the most painful perception that one doesn't want to know anything about.

The term *Verleugnung* had been used previously by Freud in 1915 in the article *Thoughts for the Times on War and Death*, where he used it in reference to how the setting off of the World War I substantially changed man's attitude toward death. It reads, "It is evident that war is bound to sweep away this conventional treatment of death. Death will no longer be denied; we are forced to believe in it" (1957a, 291).

In another essay from the same period, *A Metapsychological Supplement to the Theory of Dreams*, which is contemporary to *Mourning and Melancholia*, while reflecting on the elemental phenomena of hallucinations that occur as a result of a loss that is intolerable for the self, he describes an entity known as hallucinatory psychosis of desire, or the amentia of Meynert. He defines it as a state of acute delirium where, hallucinatorily, the object that reality affirms is lost, is recovered. Thus, the examination of reality is partially canceled. This clinical entity, in 1894, had been a subsidiary of the mechanism of *Verwerfung* (foreclosure).[9] In said text, he gives the examples of a mother, alienated by the death of her son, who cradles a block of wood in her arms, and a jilted bride that waits for the groom all spruced up every day for years.

We mentioned those places were Freud used the term *Verleugnung* to propose the hypothesis that, faced with that which never ceases to not register—sex and death—the former on account of the difference and radical disagreement between the sexes, and the latter as the loss of the loved object—the subject responds at first with denial. They temporarily cancel the so-called "reality testing."

We see then that said mechanism, *Verleugnung*, proves useful for us to think about the irruption of phenomena distinct from the symptoms, but within the structure of neurosis. Those phenomena are often spoken of as partial foreclosures. Seeing as we are considering them as part of the structure of neurosis, we believe it's more relevant to regard them as disavowed phenomena. Lacan, when he addressed the topic of mourning during his Seminar VI, *Desire and Its Interpretation* (1958–1959), based the misplacement of Prince Hamlet's desire and the postponement of the act (Claudius's assassination) that would restore his place in the lineage on his curtailing the periods of mourning for his father, the King. He then describes—referring to the apparition of his father as a hallucination—a mechanism diametrically opposed to that of psychosis, that is, to *Verwerfung*.

Both *Verwerfung* and *Verleugnung* are mechanisms that are susceptible to producing hallucinations. When it comes to the former, namely the structure of psychosis, that which is rejected in the symbolic—Name-of-the-Father—reappears in the real, which produces the hallucinatory effect. When the latter mechanism dictates, as is the case for mourning, it's the surprising encounter with the real—the hole in existence that brings about the loss—that stirs the whole symbolic system. That is how hallucinatory phenomena arise. What's lacking is always lacking in its place. When it loses its placement, the symbolic order is disturbed, and diverse phenomena make their appearance. We believe, then, that in this first period of mourning, the operating mechanism which produces said clinical manifestations is *Verleugnung*.

The subject is dispatched, in that first moment of bereavement, to a position of deprivation, deprivation of coming to grips with what's lacking. It's a time of phantasmatic vacillation. If the relationship of the subject with the signifier needs the structuring of desire by means of the phantasm, then it's this relationship that is shocked when what's lacking loses its place.

It's not unusual to discover impeded mourning in the statement of sufferings from those that come to us during their processing. A lot of times there's almost a total absence of registration of that "before and after" that a significant loss results in. That's why it's important that in the analysis method, the statement of a painful loss be registered.

What are the interventions that the analyst can employ in an effort to make that moment register instead of the subject succumbing to denial? Are there any available tools that, without being disconnected from the signifier, permit us to reach the dimension of the analytical act?

Given that the practice that compromises us prioritizes the individual nature of each case to reflect on the clinical analysis, I will refer to material that, facing the difficulties present when going through that first period of mourning, called me to a particular intervention.

SPELLING OUT THE LOSS, REGISTERING THE ABSENCE

Alba is a young, thirty-year-old working woman that came to me because she felt distressed, depressed, and with serious difficulties in her work environment. With regards to her body, she said she periodically suffered from terrible headaches—"I feel like my head is going to split in two"—and serious menstrual disorders that caused severe hemorrhages (endometriosis for which she had to undergo four surgeries).

She is the daughter of a judge who's well-known, where she's from, for his *irreproachable conduct*, using the patient's words. Alba distinguished herself through high grades while she was in school, and later for her respectable professional practice in a number of diverse law offices that she worked in.

Nonetheless, at the moment that she's doing the consultation, she's about to quit her job, even though it is considerably interesting to her. It became unbearable for her to continue going after starting a controversial romantic relationship with a colleague from her office. The issue was that it was a man who's considerably older than her, and whose wife called Alba everyday, torturing her with threats and scandals.

She mentioned that her dad passed away recently from aggressive liver cancer. I asked her when, and she said, "One year ago . . ." She corrected herself, " . . . no, two." I insisted, "when?" She couldn't even remember the year, the month, or the day. In fact, she was surprised and asked, "Why does that even matter?"

I responded that it probably had more importance than she thought.

In the following appointment, she told me how she couldn't take it at work anymore, and that she was going to take a leave of absence. Having already requested medical leave on two occasions in a short period of time, and faced with the difficulty of reintegrating herself into the workplace, she decided to quit, coinciding with the end of the year. She announced that she would be traveling to Spain for a while, visiting a friend that lived over there.

On one occasion where I took a few minutes to open the door of the office, by the time I opened it, she had already left. Later, she explained that she couldn't wait, that she felt the need to leave.

There were only a few appointments with Alba after that since she subsequently left on her trip. However, after a few months she returned, and, alluding to a saying, expressed somewhat slyly, "It's like when we came back from Spain."

The sessions went by seized by silence, or sometimes she would get up and say, "I'd rather leave. I can't talk." She would relate how she would stay inside her house for hours, or that she would hang out with people that she didn't find interesting. The biggest difficulty was when people invited her to activities related to the professional field which she had specialized in. She would thwart herself by forgetting to go and thinking that it wouldn't meet her expectations.

I often felt, after the drawn-out silences that prolonged each session, that I was accompanying someone through the pain of mourning. Someone who still couldn't articulate anything about the event, but could only compulsively leave the places that most drew her attention—a clear exhibition of acting out. She had also left her hometown after her father's death, wanting to settle down in Buenos Aires where, as a friend would tell her, *she continued being a small town girl*. She retreated into herself, staying inside her apartment, or she lived going out, not being able to appropriate for herself any space. Comparing her childhood and adolescence in her hometown and the prestigious place her family had in that setting with the capital, where nobody knew her, she related nostalgically how everything "that was known had passed to become anonymous." At which point I commented that from anonymity, it's very difficult to become recognized. It was an intervention aiming at recovering identificatory marks, recalling coordinates within her history from which she could find a place, and contextualizing her desire of settling down in Buenos Aires.

How could onc intervene faced with such immutable silence? What strategy could one apply where transference seems to have settled in, but not analysis? She routinely came to the sessions twice a week. Repeatedly, like a preamble to the silence, she would start the session with, "Everything's the same."

Generally, upon asking about or noting something regarding the huge family breakdown—in several aspects, including economically—that the death of her father meant, she would comment that she preferred not to talk about it.

On one occasion, when the silence was heavy, I turned on the computer and started to print something. With the monotonous background noise the machine made while printing I commented, "It must be that after some point *nothing was the same*." *A posteriori* I understood that the printer made the silence evident. It made the silence heard, but it also referred to the registration of a text, faced with a tendency to permanent subjective fainting. It probably also signaled that the peculiar act of the analyst wagered on an awakening that would break the lethargy that the analysis fell into at times.

After a while, and for the first time, Alba started to cry miserably; afterward she bid me farewell until the next session. Next time she commented,

> I had never recalled it, but in my family there were people who killed themselves. My grandpa and my dad's older sister. That was never talked about in my family. On the day that my grandpa shot himself, the only thing I remember is that I was with my siblings watching TV. Then my dad entered and turned everything off, and we all just stayed there in silence.

Surprisingly, after that particular intervention—in the real—there occurred a decisive shift in the analysis. She began to remember family incidents that portrayed a father that imparted order, though on occasion with extreme severity. One time she shared a dream that brought her to ask herself about her bodily afflictions. What would be ordinary illnesses for others became an extremely grave look for her. "Why is it that when I catch a cold I almost suffocate from not being able to breathe? Why does a headache leave me bedridden for a week? Why do menstrual pains send me to the operating room?"

What we consider a logical second period of mourning materialized. A lot of time and energy would be spent here, and it's described in the renowned essay *Mourning and Melancholia* as the piece by piece detachment of the libido to the lost object by means of remembrance.

We had proposed to link the concept of *Verleugnung* with the first period of mourning, the stage where the implosion within the structure dispatches the subject to a position of deprivation where the subject prefers to disavow, to deny taking notice of the loss. This work is not the opportunity to get into the analysis of the logical periods of mourning, which carries out the different phantasmatic positions of the subject with regards to the lost object. Nonetheless, I wanted to highlight that the two previously mentioned periods would culminate in a third period, where the self declares the object dead. In other words, the subject assumes an active role with regards to the separation, and they recover their libido. What had been experienced passively as abandonment now reverts into an active stance that declares the object dead for a second time. Thus, the libido then returns to the self, and the absence is restored. The dialectic of desire is once again mobilized.

We recognize the function of mourning in fundamentally supporting the formation of desire. When the logic that advances its elaboration halts, it's possible to observe in clinical studies effects from their narcosis by the generalized inhibitions proper to mourning with melancholic demeanor or expressions of their deviation to normal behavior as is the case with repeated acting out.

If Freud talks about the substitution of the object as the culmination of mourning's work, we understand that Lacan proposes in the last class of the Seminar X, *Anxiety* (1962–1963), resuming what had been said in previous seminars, not only its development, but also a function of mourning. A function that would consist of carrying out the transition from action as being purely a game of repeated acting out to that which acquires action status.

The fact that the function is fulfilled would entail not only the substitution of other objects of the world for the lost object, but also the transformation of the phantasmatic position with respect to the object. At that point where the object is irreplaceable, mourning, through the significant recomposition that it implies, promotes the registration of a new, personal path. The limits that the subject was previously confined to because of the psychic pain become the passport to a position that's less inhibited and less conducive to the realization of desired acts.

NOTES

1. To find antecedents of this term that characterized both a sickly condition as well as the temperament of men labeled as having a certain level of spiritual greatness, see Klibansky, Panofsky, & Saxl. 1979. *Saturn and Melancholy*. Liechtenstein: Kraus Reprint.
2. Lacan uses this term "formal envelope" to define the symptom in his writing *On My Antecedents*. There he says, "For faithfulness to the symptom's formal envelope, which is the true clinical trace for which I acquired a taste, led me to the limit at which it swings back in creative effects" (Lacan 2006, 52).
3. Since what is at the nucleus of the distinction between mourning and melancholy is the phantasmatic position of the subject with respect to the object, we propose, following Freud, calling it melancholy when the object that has been lost has not been identified, and calling it *melancholized mourning* when it's stopped during its process. In the latter, though the lost object can be individualized, it's far from entering the path to registering as an absence in the structure.
4. See Freud, S. 1961a. *Neurosis and Psychosis*.
5. Taken from the dissertation of Victoria H. Julia published as the introduction in *La tragedia griega* [The Greek Tragedy] Buenos Aires: Plus Ultra, 1993.
6. That's what Lacan calls the (φ) in his Seminar X, *Anxiety* (1962–1963), class on 11/28/62.
7. *Ibidem* (class on 7/2/63).
8. See chapter 2.
9. It's worth it to remark that said mechanism, which Lacan would later designate as specific to psychosis, was first used by Freud to allude to the production of hallucinatory phenomena in the field of pathological grief.

BIBLIOGRAPHY

Aries, P. 2008. *The Hour of Our Death*. New York: Random House.

Freud, S. 1957a. "Mourning and Melancholia" in *The Standard Edition of the Complete Psychological Works of Sigmund Freud [SE], Vol. XIV*. London: The Hogarth Press, 237–58.

Freud, S. 1957b. "Thoughts for the Times on War and Death," in *SE, Vol. XIV*, London: The Hogarth Press, 273–300.

Freud, S. 1961a. "Neurosis and Psychosis" in *SE, Volume XIX*, London: The Hogarth Press, 149–53.

Julia, V. 1993. *La tragediagriega* [The Greek Tragedy]. Buenos Aires: Plus Ultra.

Klibansky, R., Panofsky, E. &Saxl, F. 1979. *Saturn and Melancholy*¸ Liechtenstein: Kraus Reprint.Lacan, J. 2006. "On My Antecedents" in *Écrits: The First Complete Edition in English*. New York: Norton & Co., 51–56.

Lacan, J. 2014. *Anxiety: The Seminar of Jacques Lacan, Book X*. Cambridge: Polity Press.

Chapter 2

The Subjectivating Function of Mourning

FROM *TRAUERARBEIT* TO THE SUBJECTIVATING FUNCTION

"In what does the work of mourning consist?" Lacan asked when he picked up the clearly Freudian tradition in his Seminar VI, *Desire and Its Interpretation* (1958–1959).[1] Perhaps it wouldn't even be an exaggeration to say that Freud wrote *Mourning and Melancholia* to answer, essentially, the said question. Throughout the text, he proceeds to present successive logical periods through which a person in mourning goes through. Right from the start, where what prevails is the mechanism of denial or disavowal—"I know . . . but still"—to a posthumous moment where, after victimizing the object, that is, accomplishing for a second instance the loss caused by the loved object, the libido would be available for investing in other objects.

Mourning is probably one of the most widespread experiences in the human plane. From the moment of its birth, the speaking self-initiates a path of alienation and separation from the objects of the world which is edifying for their subjectivity. The social and cultural expressions that mourning promotes represent the attitude of mankind toward death in different civilizations in different ages.

Thus, there is an intersection between the elaboration of a loss in the singularity of each case and the way in which a certain community or collective structure orients itself faced with the conceptualization of death.

Mourning, as we read from Freud's pen, is that normal reaction to a loss of a loved one or of an equivalent abstraction: one's homeland, liberty, ideals. Nonetheless, even though it's a normal reaction, Freud proposes to effect a work—*Trauerarbeit.*[2] It is, then, a work that implies a considerable expenditure of time and energy for the psychic apparatus. It's a demand of work that, if it lingers in any of the logical periods of elaboration, leads to various clinical manifestations.

We understand that three different logical periods can be established in the elaboration of mourning; periods to traverse the pain caused by the loss of the loved object. A first period is where the mechanism that operates is denial—*Verleugnung*. We know of the reluctance of the young human to admit that something loved has abandoned them. Apparitions of the loved one will proliferate, then, in different phenomenal ways: illusions where they believe that they hear or see the dead, and sometimes having hallucinations. A second period where, slowly, and after a great expenditure of time and money, piece by piece, through remembering and elaborating, ceremonies and rituals, reuniting with objects that had belonged to or represented the one who had passed away—the relics—a significant recomposition occurs with respect to what was lost. And a third period which will permit the culmination of the work of mourning. The subject, after that arduous task, is able to effect the loss for a second time, or to lose in the symbolic what they had lost in the real. In opposition to the first period, now the self can declare the object as lost, and thus appease the wrath generated in the self. In this way the libido is once again available to invest in other objects that replace the loss.

But it would be quite naïve to think that the object which we are mourning is replaceable. As we were saying before, whoever is mourning carries out the loss by supplementing it with a small piece of themselves, a sacrificial status of mourning that manifests itself in the most diverse forms of expressing and manifesting the pain.

The object which we are mourning was a loved object, with the relief of the narcissistic choice which every romantic relationship is comprised of. As a popular song rightly asserts, they are "what we were missing"—support for the structural fault, and for whom we can utter "I was their missing piece," since we know that we love with what we don't have.

Accordingly, bereavement is the occasion where the aforementioned significant recomposition that entails the elaboration of the loss constitutes itself the fertile ground to subjectivize the loss, that is, to elevate it to the category of lack. The function of mourning is not the replacement of the object, but the transformation of the relationship between the subject and the phantasmatic object.

In that stretch, where the function of mourning consists of subjectivizing the loss, that section where the object isn't replaceable because it's labeled as unique, advancing in the work of mourning implies supplementing, with a new piece, digging up their own creative feature to where the shine of the object isn't too dazzling nor the weight of its shadow overpower the new piece. In short, with that real boost that the message of mourning contributes to compose a different piece.

Making use of the homonymous property of the term *duelo*, which comes from two Latin roots, one of which is *dolus* (pain) and the other *duellum* (challenge), as was mentioned in the previous chapter, we can say that mourning is a psychic pain, sorrow, and affliction, but also a challenge to the structure. It's a challenge to produce the signifying recomposition that allows the subject to make the instituting lack available, recreating it.

In mourning, the subject identifies themselves with the loved object while lost. Dominated by that identification, the subject also loses themselves in some sense. They become disoriented; they go astray.

There are diverse ways that the avatars of halted, impeded, or restricted mourning can be clinically expressed. We previously mentioned depressive mood, generalized inhibition, abulia, and disinterest marked by everything foreign to the lost object. They are manifestations that, when dragged out, impart melancholic nuances. We also profile along with these manifestations other ones that can appear like eating disorders (bulimia, anorexia), addictions (alcohol, drugs), and psychosomatic illnesses. On occasion, *agieren*, behaving or acting impulsively, dominates the scene, and we find modes of action that are disjointed from desires as is the case for permanent, repetitive acting out, or the *passage à l'acte*.

It's at this point that I would like to stop for a moment and highlight that, just as it is detected in clinical studies, Lacan emphasized the relationship between acting out and the function of mourning. When the latter doesn't proceed, being a crucial link in the pathway to desire, the action appears as inhibited, and in its place acting out abounds. What is the link that could be made between acting out, the function of mourning, and action?

In the Seminar X, *Anxiety* (1962–1963),[3] Lacan presented in the first class a matrix where he places, diagonally, inhibition, symptom, and anguish. In the remaining cells he placed the following terms: emotion, turmoil, impediment, and embarrassment. Two cells remained empty. They would later be occupied by acting out and *passage à l'acte*. As the seminar proceeded, he replaced the terms inside the cells.

One of these would remain empty, and in it, near the end of the seminar, Lacan places acting out. In the following class, the one on July 3, 1963, he says,

> What we are going to place at the level of acting-out is the function of mourning in so far as in a moment I'll be asking you to recognize here what in a previous year I taught you to see in terms of a fundamental structure of the constitution of desire. (Lacan 2014, 333)

He was referring to what he posed in Seminar VI, *Desire and Its Interpretation* (1958–1959), where he details the avatars of unbound action

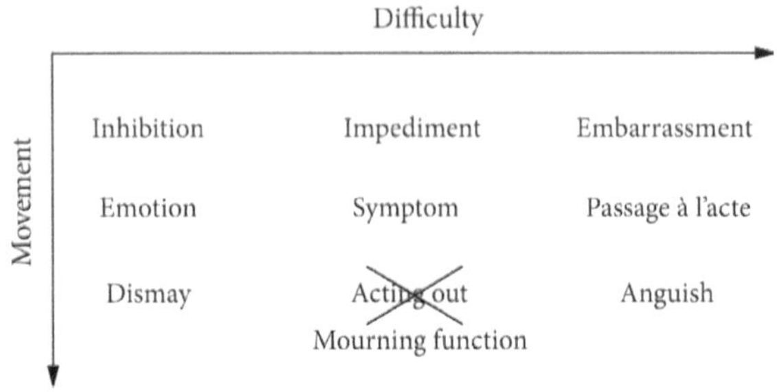

Figure 2.1 Table of Seminar X, Anxiety (1962–1963). *Source:* Created by the author.

of desire in the play, *Hamlet*. As a result of the vicissitudes of mourning his father, he rightly called the play the "tragedy of desire."

The fact that funeral ceremonies are shorter is evidence of this, since, as the script ironically points out, the repast also served for the celebration of the wedding between Gertrude, Hamlet's mom, and Claudius, the uncle that usurped the throne. Freud had already noted the ups and downs that the young prince goes through from that moment on. In *The Interpretation of Dreams*, he emphasizes that Hamlet wasn't incapable of taking action. He then describes two occasions where he acted decisively: one time where, in a passionate outburst, he kills the spy hiding behind a tapestry, and the other time when he kills two couriers that had the mission of ending his life. Freud emphasized that Hamlet can take action with regards to anything except for vengeance against the man that has usurped, both on the throne and in the marital bed, his father's place, that is, that which shows him the realization of his infantile oedipal desires.

Lacan places the impediment of committing the act of revenge, the vicissitudes so that the mourning operates by serving its function, as an essentially subjectivating function in the sense of reregistering the loss and propelling the desire on the pathway to action. Hamlet's drive oscillates between rashness and procrastination. It's a permanent *agieren*, subordinated by the Other.

Instances of acting out occur one after the other, from the accidental assassination of Polonius, to a trip that Hamlet takes where he almost loses his life. It was only when faced with the deadly dagger that he could carry out the action—killing Claudius—that would avenge his father and restore his place in the monarchic line. The desubjectivation in play degrades, nonetheless, the action to a *passage à l'acte*.

The work of mourning would have as a function to trade in a drive linked to acting out and *passage à l'acte*, or the generalized inhibition characteristic of pathological mourning, for a drive linked to the action, the action as an effect of a determined desire.

Now we know that having action status doesn't necessarily imply taking action, much less movement. In fact, nothing is less similar to an action than a knee-jerk reaction. The extent of the action involves the significant and has a legality at play, a registration. It implies crossing a threshold by which something new is born.

The work of elaboration that mourning entails is not unrelated to a recomposition of the signifying order which leads to a subjectivating function for the person who goes through it. It's a function that is closely linked to the act of naming, producing, and creating a name for that immeasurable unknown that death brings about for the subject.

Without a doubt, the artistic manifestations of different orders frequently reflect the necessary processing of pooled pain into the unknowable of the inexorable sunset. Especially those linked to written art model the attempt to grapple with, contextualize, and establish order within the abyss and chaos of death. The phrases, the verses, the goodbyes written on the immutable marble or resistant bronze on a tombstone are faithfully representative allusions of the attempt to register the ineffable. Among these, the poetic act, maybe, with the metaphoric flight that its style contains, is the one that most favors a deed that, in treating the impossible, designates how unmentionable the loss is.

THE FOURTH PERIOD OF MOURNING: THE SUPPLEMENTARY

We previously said that during the lecture that Lacan gave on the mourning in the tragedies of *Antigone* and *Hamlet*, that he brought to light a rationale that alludes to the consideration of the process of formulating the loss which results in devastating consequences for the protagonists, since it involves their own death, in the outcome of the plot.

We found that outcome at the end of *Mourning and Melancholia*, by which the subject, having advanced in processing their mourning, would be in condition to produce for a second time the loss from an active position—we would add that it would be the way to register it as missing—which would permit them to retrieve the libido from the object that was lost and invest it in other objects.

Substituting the lost object with other objects, having the libido find an anchor for the subjective movement to new bonds, just as the aforementioned text proposes, seems highly auspicious. Nonetheless, the object which the subject is mourning for is irreplaceable—we know the amount of narcissistic libido that is mobilized around an affective choice—whereby the shortcut we find in Freud is that it's resolved through a series of infinite substitutions. Evidently, Freud finds, as he himself states while concluding the article, that there are still serious difficulties in responding to the question that forms the backbone of this text: Why is it that when faced with an irreparable loss, some subjects go through mourning while others succumb to melancholia?

That is why, and this appears to me to be the key point, to detect why the notion of substitution doesn't resolve the problem, we need to emphasize that the lost object is not replaceable.

What I mean to say is that there are some losses that make a hole in the real. Those that were the support of the absence, of the desiring phantasmatic position of a subject. A loss that disrupts the referent symbolic universe of a subject can submerge them in a melancholized, stagnated mourning. If they advance through the periods of the elaboration of mourning, they'll be able to process the loss and supplant the lost object with a new one, or an infinite series of objects will replace it.

The concept of supplements offers a third alternative. Supplementing the loss implies doing something different with the lost object. Bereavement would offer the occasion where, in the signifier recomposition that it entails through the remembrance when detaching from the object piece by piece, to the point where the object is irreplaceable, something new is registered. Supplementation is a detotalization, which operates in excesses, forcing to register something new and altering the logical chain in which it's registered. It constrains the subject in an almost violent manner to extract some pertinent signifier to be named, to spell out the singular object of their mourning. It forces them to emerge from the submission to the object, whose weight looms over them and to expose to the maximum their condition as the subject. That's why mourning, in addition to the depressive nature it entails as such, is an occasion for recomposing the absence and producing a liberating separation that opens up the possibility of an act, understood as a creative act.

In some form or fashion there's an association with the Freudian term "sublimation." It's a logical fourth period of mourning, tangential to the notion of supplementarity. If Freud proposes the period where the loss is consummated for a second time, thereby withdrawing the libido from the lost object and investing it in other objects, Lacan wagers and emphasizes the production of a change in the subjective position in relation to the object. A shift begins to occur from the lost object toward the objects that functions as the source in the structure because it's fundamentally about the lack in the Other, of the object essentially absent.

This concept of supplements is not unconcerned with the feminine. We know that it's the term that Lacan uses to refer to woman's own enjoyment (*jouissance*). Therefore, maybe it wouldn't be wrong to think that accessing this fourth period of mourning, the supplementary one, involves the feminine condition. It's about finding the supplementarity of an enjoyment that's concerned with the letter and the writing.[4]

A Clinical Case of an Unannounced Death

Diana is now forty-seven years old. She has a degree in Sociology and two kids. Dissatisfied, she has been going in for consultation for several years, essentially because she can't find a job in her field. At that time, she worked selling gift items. Her general malaise was accompanied by intestinal pains and disorders, which had been diagnosed as irritable bowel syndrome, and which on occasion had forced her to stay in bed. Her mom had passed away when she was fourteen years old, just a few days before they planned move to a floor (TN: flat)—which was how she addressed that upscale apartment that her family fatefully never ended up living in. It was an unexpected and almost inexplicable death, which according to the family lore of some aunts was because they envied her, or that she was poisoned due to a syrup she took because of intestinal parasites, from the medical point of view.

It was a flat she never got to live in, and which in her adolescence left without a floor to stand on. An unannounced death that suddenly disrupted the course of her path.

It'd be impossible to detail several years of analysis. Thus, I will relate this moment of analysis which, in some way, says something about her changes of subjective position. It had already been several years since she had been on track to advance in her career in a branch she had been developing. In view of the presentation of the first issue of a magazine that she ran, at the end of a session she asked herself who she'd invite to such an event, for which she had been preparing herself with a lot of expectations.

When she returned for the following session, she mentioned that she had been thinking about it, and that she had sat down to put together a list of those that she wanted to attend, and that suddenly she felt a chill and cry. It crossed her mind that they were the same ones that she would want to come and greet her in her last farewell, at her funeral.

Mourning impeded in its moments of elaboration frequently, and in a completely unconscious manner, pushes the subject to sacrifice and procrastinate, to inhibit advancing along the path of desire, to boycott themselves, to play as if they were on the opposing team, to not allow themselves what in reality is accessible.

The second death: the area where death insinuates itself into life. It's the moment of the periods of mourning that authorizes us to talk about the clinical study of mourning that promotes an encounter with castration, while a limit, finite.

We don't believe that mourning necessarily carries with it a quota of sacrifice for the subject. As the definition indicates, the sacrifice refers to imposing deprivations on oneself as an offering to another. The sacrifice, with the connotations it carries, would be precisely what detains the bereavement in deprivation.

Going through mourning on occasion becomes the opportunity to transform the phantasmatic position with respect to the object, in order to register a new round for the operation of castration, abandoning the deprived stance.

For mourning to not be impeded in the substitution of a lost object for another one that has been conquered, metonymically, and a subjectivation of the loss arise where the supplementary relieves what's merely substitutional, the modification has to operate on the level of the object itself, the object produced by the structure. It would once again be about the bid to elevate the object to the grade of "the thing." It'd be about opening the path to a supplementary enjoyment, beyond the phallic enjoyment.

THE ISSUE OF MOURNING AND THE STATUS OF THE OBJECT

From the Navel of the Dream to the "Object a"

The issue of mourning is entrenched in the conceptualization of the object for psychoanalysis. With the invention of the *object a* by Lacan, any attempt to assign the object an ontological or substantial status to the object is blurred. Naming the object with a letter of the alphabet, "a"—as Lacan calls his invention—sweeps away any pretense to grant the object some consistency.

It recovers the coordinates of complexity for psychoanalytic theory with those that Freud had defined when he mentioned it as "das Ding"—the Thing—in *Project for a Scientific Psychology* (1895)[5] or "navel of the dream" to designate the impenetrable nucleus that dreaming dwells in.

In the *Project*, "das Ding" corresponds to that which is implacable and incapable of being articulated in the process of judging. It represents a radical otherness for the subject. It's the void that, being outside of all signification, enables the articulation of the chain of representations. It's the impossible reunion.[6]

The treatment of the concept of the object in the "Appendix C: Words and Things" in José Etcheverry's Spanish translation of the article *The Unconscious* is highly interesting. Without going into it deeply, it's worth remembering that there the representation-object is affirmed to be an open complex which could hardly be closed, while the representation-words appears to us to be something closed, though susceptible to enlargement.

Frequently, post-Freudian psychoanalysts tended to ontologize and give consistency to the concept of the object, more often than not personalizing it in the figure of the fathers as the first objects of love.

A large part of the theory of mourning revolved around the reestablishment of the lost objects in the ego. It was sustained that each advancement in the process of mourning resulted in the deepening of the relationship between the individual and their internal objects, to reconquer and recover them in the ego.

Mourning and its distinction from depression and melancholia was a topic that the post-Freudian analysts dedicated themselves to extensively. I will briefly mention the developments of some of them like Karl Abraham and Melanie Klein.

The first one[7] disseminates the concept of the partial object systemizing the theory of the libido, which culminates in accessing the love of a complete object in the genital phase. It affirms that in normal mourning, the subject accomplishes restoring the loved person that was lost in the ego, whereas the melancholic fails in that attempt. Abraham places the emphasis on the loss of the object as the triggering factor in melancholia, but he highlights the importance of the constitutional with a fixation on the libido in the oral phase and the regression to infantile narcissism. The melancholic can't work out the loss through mourning because they tend to eliminate the object as they would feces. They later narcissistically identify themselves with the object and take their revenge on them by tormenting themselves. This occurs on the basis of a double introjection of the lost object in the ego and superego.

For M. Klein,[8] a close connection existed between mourning and the processes of early childhood. The child passes through mental states comparable to the bereavement of adults, and it's these early bereavements that serve them later in life when they experience something distressing. It affirms that in both normal and pathological mourning, as well as manic-depressive states, the depressive infantile position is reactivated. She proposes that the fundamental difference between normal mourning on one hand and pathological mourning and manic-depressive states on the other is the following: those suffering from bipolar disorder and the subjects that fail during the work of mourning have in common the inability during their early childhood to establish good internal objects. Conversely, normal mourning consists in the subject reinstalling within themselves their real lost objects of love and at the same time their first loved objects, ultimately, their good parents. It's these who, when the real loss occurred, the subject was also afraid of losing.

This author makes the possibility of the elaboration of the loss revolve around the capacity that the subject had in their early childhood to establish good internal objects, at a time when the breast covers the hegemony of the object relations.

Other authors[9] emphasize the differentiation between the normal and pathological qualities of mourning. They make this distinction based on the existence of two classes of guilt. The persecutory guilt that faces the object and the ego will determine the appearance of pathological mourning, which frequently culminate in melancholic conditions or other psychotic expressions. On the other hand, depressive guilt, when it manages to free itself from its persecutory components, creates the possibility for an authentic repair of the ego.

As can be deduced from the previous development, the work of mourning for these authors would consist in reestablishing, reinstating, and restoring once again the lost object in the ego as a result of the work of the processing of the loss.

These developments on the topic of mourning and melancholia support the theorization of the object linked to a series of representations; it's an object defined by a phenomenal materiality.

When Lacan expounds on the topic of the object in psychoanalysis,[10] he firstly introduces a thorough critique of the previously mentioned formulations, remembering that in following Freud, we can't disregard the notion of the lack of object as central in the exercise of analytical theory, as the motor of the relationship of the subject with the world.

He insists on remembering the formula presented in *Project for a Scientific Psychology*, in which the object of satisfaction is always an object that's been recovered from one that's been lost. Thus, by mere repetition discord is introduced, that is, by structure the object is the lack of an object. The primacy of this dialectic introduces a deep tension in the center of the subject–object relationship in such a way that what is sought isn't sought in the same way as that which is found. The new object is searched for through the pursuit of a past satisfaction, in both senses of the word, and it's found elsewhere that the point at which it is sought.[11] The *object a* is the object that is definitely lost; the void that the drive doesn't stop contouring. It's the part that, torn from the Other, constitutes the subject's own loss. The *object a* isn't a natural object of the body; it's produced in the real loss of the signifying articulation. The "surplus of enjoyment," the *object a* presents that irrecoverable loss of enjoyment that the sexuated mortal suffers.[12]

The dialectic between the subject and object isn't about basing the analytical progress on the finding of an object that's fully satisfactory, harmonious, and adequate for the subject's maturity. Instead, it's based on going around the borders of the hole that the lack of an object plows through the subjective structure. It's about, then, advancing to the edge of the lack's capacity, hinging on the castration of the subject and of the Other, avoiding to plug—by closing or clogging—the instituting dearth of the speaking being with some object materiality.

Without a doubt, these two conceptions of the object in psychoanalysis divide the waters in an incisive way that carries with it important consequences regarding the direction that treatment takes.

Thinking of the lack of object as central to the dialectic between the subject and the drive's circuit ascribes analysis as operative for access or penetration in the real that affects a subject in how they deal with the modalities of enjoyment.

With regards to the elaboration of mourning and the logical periods of how it's processed—which is the topic at hand—we consider that there is a stark difference in how the direction of an analysis is affected according to how one theorization or another of the object is conceived.

Let's remember that Freud, in *Mourning and Melancholia*, emphasized that mourning consists in authenticating the loss of the object piece by piece, sign by sign, ideal by ideal, gradually, with a great expenditure of time and energy. He says,

> Reality-testing has shown that the loved object no longer exists, and it proceeds to demand that all libido shall be withdrawn from its attachments to that object. This demand arouses understandable opposition—it is a matter of general observation that people never willingly abandon a libidinal position, not even, indeed, when a substitute is already beckoning to them. . . . Each single one of the memories and expectations in which the libido is bound to the object is brought up and hypercathected, and detachment of the libido is accomplished in respect of it. (Freud, 1957a, 244–45)

Mourning entails the arduous labor of libidinal dehiscence of the lost object, a labor which will allow the subject to later invest libidinally in other objects. On that road of libidinal detachment, the subject incorporates traits of the loved object in the unconscious eagerness of retaining them. It should be noted that attenuated identifications claim strong prominence in these circumstances. This identification with the object's traits obeys the registration of the principle of reality that asserts that the object no longer is. It's a preliminary acceptance of the absence and not an adequate recovery of the object in the ego. That's why we insist that mourning is the occasion to revisit the inexorable lack of objects that engenders it while a subject. In other words, mourning is the exquisite and unique opportunity, a challenge to the structure, to rediscover the inaugural lack of the subjective condition, and to even display it.

Between Lights and Shadows

In melancholia, "the shadow of the object fell upon the ego" (Freud 1957a, 249). The subject vests each object of the world that they choose with agalmatic shine. We can say that those objects that come to occupy a space in the phantasm shine with a phallic shine. This stays directly proportional to the shadow that descends when they part, distance themselves, or perish. That's where the narcissistic commitment of the idealized choice resides. When we ask ourselves what is lost when the object is lost, we find that it's the libidinal, narcissistic economy. The light that illuminated the ego is extinguished by the object. That's the point where the ways of processing the losses that inevitably occur throughout the course of life will differ.

What is it that brings along the decrease in sense of self or self-esteem characteristic of melancholic humor? The necessity of punishment and self-reproach. While in mourning it's the world that has become diminished, in melancholia or melancholized mourning it's the ego which has become completely diminished, shrunken.

This need of punishment manifests itself in diverse and repetitive ways when bereavements don't proceed through the necessary periods of registration, of spelling out the trauma. The compulsion to repeat, repeats. They repeat desertions, embody illnesses, and endure pains and paralyzing inhibitions. It's criminal in the destructive sense of death, but what they attempt unsuccessfully—such that they fail and it continues to repeat—is something that is inscribed; it's imprinted on the structure.

Faced with the clinical manifestations of mourning, which present themselves through diverse phenomena, the wager is that they register in the coordinates of what's symptomatic. In other words, it's under the aegis of repression, an operation that's obstructed when the subject denies the relationship they had with what was lost.

The need of punishment, which exposes the subject to expressing their mourning sacrificially, on occasion manifests itself embodied by psychosomatic phenomena, sometimes bringing them to the brink of death, as is the case with cancer, or being taken by a death in life, as is the case with melancholia. It also ensnares them in permanent contradictory actions where they cause serious accidents, or they volunteer themselves to be cheated in various scenarios in their lives. The desperate attempts to swallow the object by recurring to drinking, drug consumption, or excessive eating are other manifestations of the bereavements.

The brush with the real produces a phantasmatic collapse. The real, which isn't reality, has a point of contact with it. It's that part of reality that comes in contact with the innermost fiber of the subject. Death is one of the faces of the real that gives free rein to the drive, the deadly, disentwined drive. There isn't anything symbolic or imaginary that can come to anticipate the impact of the real. Nothing that can state just how hazardous said meeting is. There is no *a priori* knowledge.

When, following Lacan, we say that the hole of the loss that mourning causes in the real, which isn't reality as we just suggested, we understand that it's the real of the fabric, that which comes in contact with the tissue of the subjective structure. It's that which is concerned with the centerpoint where subjectivity stumbles, and that, reducing light, glooms melancholically.

Mourning and Anguish

In the last point of the appendix of *Inhibitions, Symptoms, and Anguish* (Freud 1959a), aptly called "Anxiety, Pain and Mourning," Freud intends to clear up the difference between said concepts.

He had already defined mourning in 1915 as the normal reaction when faced with the loss of a loved person, or to the loss of some abstraction which has taken the place of one, such as one's country, liberty, or an ideal. How does he define anguish? The subtle difference with anguish is that it's the reaction to the danger, the threat, of the loss of an object, the object of satisfaction, the mother. But it isn't the gestating mother, the birth mother—it's not about the anguish of birth which Otto Rank proposes—but the mother object created through repeated situations of satisfaction where they were the protagonist.

The well-known aphorism "anguish is not without object" (Lacan 2014, 242) gives an answer to that Freudian reflection. The object has to have been constituted for the threat of losing it to transpire. Often this statement seems to encapsulate a paradoxical nuance. Isn't it true that anguish presents itself in the face of the threat of the loss of the object? How can we link it so closely to its presence? Nonetheless, the signal anguish, which serves to warn and guide the subject, doesn't deploy its effectiveness without the object, the object *a*, first having been engendered within the structure.

Some years after 1915, Freud once again began to ponder this term to which he indubitably imprinted a psychoanalytic tradition in *Inhibition, Symptoms, and Anguish*. It's precisely in the appendix that he reminds us that he was unable to explain a particular trait in the 1915 text: it's peculiar painfulness. Trying to provide a counterpoint with the concepts of anguish and psychic pain, he takes up a question that he says he left hanging in suspense, "why does mourning hurt?" He introduces pain to define when the separation from an object produces anguish and when it results in mourning. Recognizing the pain opens the door to designating the object of interest and beginning the work of mourning. Anguish defers to a subjective upheaval, where the threat that prevails is that the rupture from the object does not occur again. In this situation, there's an overwhelming prevalence of the phantasmatic object, which sometimes impedes the pain from initiating mourning.[13]

The Mathemes of Mourning: a, i(*a*), Φ

We'll start with a phrase from the Seminar X, *Anxiety* (1962–1963):

> The problem of mourning is the problem of maintaining, at the scopic level, the bonds whereby desire is suspended, not from the object a, but from i(a), by

> which all love is narcissistically structured in so far as the term love implies the idealized dimension I spoke about. (Lacan, 2014, 335)

This paragraph links mourning to the predominant type of election of an object for which they are mourning. An essentially narcissistic election.

The maintenance of the bonds through which desire sustains the i(*a*)—the mirror image—is the essential problem. Once the object is dead, absent from the field of view, be it literally or metaphorically speaking, carrying out the separation that would allow for sustaining the mirror image upright, libidinized, and joyful is the task to be completed.

Even though the concept of the object *a*, designated as such, begins to acquire specificity throughout Seminar VI, *Desire and Its Interpretation* (1958–1959) it's in the Seminar X, *Anxiety* (1962–1963) where it acquires the prominence that we grant it in the phantasm, in it's doubled object version, caused by the desire and object surplus enjoyment with respect to the species of partial objects.

Toward the end of Seminar V, *The Formations of the Unconscious* (1957–1958), it's stated deriving it from the concept of the other, with a lowercase *a*, of the counterpart, to deal with the libidinal relation of the subject with their counterparts. He called it the small other, the little *a*; and this lowercase *a* would become what is exclusively an invention of Lacan: *the object a*.[14]

As we know, the concept of the object *a* maintains a singular complexity, which conforms its particularity. The object *a* can't be boiled down to its species. It doesn't only fulfill the function of what's leftover, disposed, or made void. It's located at the junction of the rings of the Borromean knot.

Let's stay on the topic of mourning. Lacan, following Freud, establishes that the way for the subject to connect with its objects of love is closely linked to the way in which, during the instituting moments, the object was produced within the structure. He states that a lack engendered at a previous time serves for responding to a lack generated at a later time.

In its construction, the i(*a*), the mirror image, has the *a* in parentheses. Within them we find a glimpse of the genesis of the object in relation to the small other, the counterpart.

A recurring definition of the object *a* is that it sustains the relation of the subject with what they are not, since they aren't the phallus. The object *a*, while a lack, supports the relationship between the subject and the imaginary castration. The mirror image of the subject, the i(*a*), is a product of that operation in which the phallus is subtracted made negative. It reads as $(-\varphi)$. From here stems the basic junction and separation between the object *a* and $(-\varphi)$. If the object *a* is operating in the subjective structure in the dimension of its complexity, stabilizing the phantasm, then the i(*a*) conforms to the mirror image of which the imaginary phallus remains necessarily subtracted.

Even though the object *a* can't be boiled down to the objects of love or idealizations which the subject chooses, nor the purported species of the object, that is, the objects that libidinize the corporal geography—breasts, feces, voice, gaze, and we could add more to the list—the way that the subject relates to the objects of the world will carry with it the unique stamp of how said object *a* was engendered in the instituting moments. To put it another way, the agalmatic shine of the chosen objects reproduces the reflection of what once was the phallic shine that had to be renounced. Through the operation of castration, the object *a* is the remains of an imprecise division. Behind the attributes of the chosen, loved object lies the object *a* in its maximum expression as the object cause of desire.

These are the objects which cause people to mourn upon losing them. One doesn't mourn for any object that's lost, or for some object that some care or attention had been given to. One mourns for the objects that encased the place of the symbolic lack. They were the support of castration in the subject. They regulated the phantasmatic position and defined their place in the world.

In the operation of the subject's coming to the place of the Other, the object *a* peels off. We can effect said writing in different ways. One is the following:

That's how the phantasm is comprised. One period is the imprecise division between the A and the S which leaves one leftover: the object *a*. Another period is the operation that will stabilize the phantasm, and which is inherent the moment the analysis ends. It consists in the subtraction of the imaginary phallus (φ), an operation between the subject and the object *a*. It's another round of imaginary castration in the subject as the effect of symbolic castration, practiced in the Other. In other words, when there isn't the Other of Other, the only thing left to do to advance the treatment is to grieve that grief of the irreparable non-existence.

It's the period of mourning that affects the ego of the subject, the very heart of the primary narcissism, transforming the position of the subject with respect to their objects.

The connotation Φ is the mark of symbolic castration in the *parlêtre*, assumed in the imaginary plane. The subtraction of the function of the imaginary phallus from the mirror image is what provides the illusion of anticipated sufficiency in their joyous encounter.

A	S
$\cancel{S}$	$\cancel{A}$
a	

Figure 2.2 Table of Subjective Division. *Source:* Created by the author.

Thus, the position of the phallus is always veiled. It appears as glow around the object. It always appears as a negative. Lacan made clear in his class on April 29, 1959 (Seminar V, *Desire and Its Interpretation,* 1958–1959) that mourning is the main route by which the loved object, having disappeared, having faded away—for a miniscule amount of time—makes it so that the true nature of what corresponds to the subject manifests itself, the appearance (*phanie* from the Greek *phainein*) of the phallus, the *phallophanies*. We believe that they correspond to the effects of depersonalization that take place, on occasion, during the initial moments of abrupt, unexpected, traumatic losses. A transitory insanity ensues with the appearance of hallucinations and delusions.

Lacan illustrates this using the appearance of the ghost of Hamlet's dead father, where he reveals to Hamlet how he had been assassinated by Claudio and then demanded to be avenged. The appearance of the ghost, while a hallucination, is an elemental phenomenon that can take place in the avatars of grief in its incipient stages. It would indicate a moment in which the phallus isn't veiled, but instead that it exerts its presence, resending the subject to a place where castration doesn't manifest itself. These apparitions of the phallus, *phallophanies*, produce a phantasmatic collapse which results in the depersonalization phenomena.

Hamlet, the famous Elizabethan play, seems to express as thoroughly as possible the vicissitudes that desire goes through during mourning. Lacan points out that Shakespeare's writing, not only in *Hamlet*, but also particularly in his sonnets, expresses with extraordinary preciseness the amorous dialectic of the subject with the object of desire. Observe the clarity with which the amorous friction that confuses the lovers' bodies is portrayed in the beautiful Sonnet XXII:

My glass shall not persuade me I am old,
So long as youth and thou are of one date;
But when in thee time's furrows I behold,
Then look I death my days should expiate.
For all that beauty that doth cover thee,
Is but the seemly raiment of my heart,
Which in thy breast doth live, as thine in me:
How can I then be elder than thou art?
O! Therefore, love, be of thyself so wary
As I, not for myself, but for thee will;
Bearing thy heart, which I will keep so chary
As tender nurse her babe from faring ill.
Presume not on thy heart when mine is slain,
Thou gav'st me thine not to give back again.[15]

We do not mourn but for those objects of which we have been their cause; swaying between love and the ideal.

Often times the subject can't identify which is the object whose loss propelled them into grief. And if he can determine which object it was, he knows whom he has lost, but not what was lost with them. This is the key that distinguishes melancholia from mourning. The latter appears to have absolute clarity on what object triggered it. Nonetheless, the widely varied clinical modalities that one who is in mourning can exhibit puts us on the path that what the subject loses with the object transcends and exceeds the object in itself. What clinical studies of melancholia show is that a reduction in the affection for themselves (the subject) perpetuates itself, or, as López Ballesteros (an Other Spanish translator) properly translates: a decrease in loving oneself. At times it doesn't seem clear in clinical phenomenology the distinction between a melancholized mourning and melancholia. Nevertheless, following Freud, in the latter permanent and unjustified self-reproaches predominate, correlated to the reduction in the affection for oneself. From the logic of the structure, that suffering and sacrificial position of the subject speaks of the inoperancy of the object in the display of its complexity and qualities. It's important that the direction of the treatment create the conditions apt for the gestation and accommodation of the object. This takes, on occasion, a long period of time, but it's crucial for the analysis to be able to begin.

The "Mourning-Desire" Cycle, the "Mania-Melancholia" Cycle

Even though mourning, with its presentation of that normal affection before a loss, is phenomenologically similar to melancholia, the essential difference lies in the decrease of love or affection for oneself, which in the latter results in the devaluation of the ego. It's a property of melancholia which on occasion reverts to its antithesis, mania. Thus, in what's termed manic-depressive psychosis, the marked difficulty of accommodating the ego is made evident, which, independently from its relation with the world, enriches or impoverishes itself cyclically.

Mourning and Melancholia, then, refers to a duality where the conjunction *and* alludes to the mode of clinical presentation. Nonetheless, its words testify to a laborious effort to provide the structural differences between that which clinical presentations put in conjunction. In the text, this is addressed from various angles to conclude that in melancholia, the object triumphs.

Effectively, in the mania-melancholia cycle the object is powerful. The subject has a sad destiny, encroached upon and reduced by the unwavering consistency of the object.

In various of Lacan's seminars, we find developments connected to situating the status that mourning has in clinical studies. We find fewer references about melancholia. But it's toward the end of the Seminar X, *Anxiety* (1962–1963) that I think I've found some contributions that are of interest for delving into said distinction.

There Lacan unfolds the conjunction and proposes what I read as an incisive distinction between the "mania-melancholia" and "mourning-desire" cycles. In the former, it's the non-function of the object *a*, and not simply its miscognition, which is at play.

Previously, at the end of the Seminar VII, *Transference* (1960–1961), there's an interesting reference about melancholia. The domain of the self-accusations, the self-reproaches, the "I am nothing," certify the remorse for "the suicide of the object" (Lacan 2015, 397). The characteristic of the gestation of the object in melancholia appears to be, according to Lacan, that of an object that has entered into the field of desire, but, because of the risk it ran in the adventure, has disappeared.

The object *a* connects the subject with what he is not: the phallus. The object *a* is the mediator. It's the operating function between what he see of themselves, their mirror image, i(*a*), and what is torn from them, in reserve (operational, libidinal reserve), a founding absence, the presence of the absence of their being in the object. We call this (Φ).

This fundamental subtraction cut out from the being is the one that leads to the illusion of a harmonic image of the body. It's an occasion of rejoicing inherent in the constitutive stage of primary narcissism. It's the real image which is accessed by the specular interplay. It's diachrony that profiles the object in the phantasm. It's the gaze of the Other that sanctions, that functions as a mirror. It's the gaze in which we look upon each other to find ourselves again: i(*a*), a paradox of an image that is real, which the subject attains by the reflection in the mirror of the gaze of the Other.

It's a moment of coagulation, of phantasmatic consistency, in which the subject is the object. It's the distortion of the image that will accomplish their accommodation once the Other rotates and gives their seat up,[16] so that the subject can redimension the place where they see themselves. These movements that constitute the matrix of primary narcissism are the ones that I propose are disjointed in the mania-melancholia cycle. It appears that the constitution of the object is aborted there.

Conversely, in the mourning-desire cycle, even though the relation with the object *a* is based on a profound lack of knowledge, with the object *a* exercising its function fully, he act as the cause frequently so that the subject can make their relationship with the lost object dialectic.

The analysis invites the work that mourning demands to also perform a function, a subjectivating function. That it register once again the absence in the place of the loss.

Thus, in analysis, the function of mourning would be to maintain the ties by which desire is stapled to the narcissistic image i(*a*), in spite of the amorous loss inflicted on the structure. Thus, the i(*a*) is the imaginary support that gives them a chance, during the split, that the loss object be replaced.

The way in which Lacan pursued the topic of mourning reveals that in its function is found the fundamental structure of the constitution of desire as decided, an act of desire. Sadness, the decline in interest and a general inhibition, as well as various clinical phenomena, can give notice of a halted work of mourning, which is therefore impeded in performing its function. Among others is the case of permanent acting out which reiterates the staging of an unfulfilled mourning. It's a succession of scenes that mounts desire, a muzzled, and thus inefficient desire, to produce the object's fall.

A set of elemental phenomena, like illusions, hallucinations, and depersonalization, as Freud has already pointed out, are also subsidiaries of the disruption of mourning in its very first phase. The *Verleugnung* phase, where the denial of the loss drags the subject away from reality to recover, through illusions or hallucinations, the loved object.

NOTES

1. See the Glossary at the end of the book for a broader explanation of *subjectivating*.
2. A German term translated as "work of mourning."
3. In his translation of Seminar X, A. R. Price states *Anxiety*as *Angoisse*. I prefer the term *Anguish* because Lacan continues the Freudian developments and enriches them with his lectures on Kierkegaard and Hegel.
4. This topic is discussed in greater detail in the section "Femininity and Mourning."
5. Das Ding subsequently appears again in Chapter III of *Totem and Taboo* and forms part of "Dingvorstellung" (representation of things) in the articles about metapsychology. (Freud 1958)
6. See Vidal, E. 1984. "A questão do objeto no campo freudiano" [The Question of the Object in the Freudian Field] in *O objetonateoria e napráticapsicanalítica*. Rio de Janeiro: Ed. Campus.
7. Abraham, K. 1927. "Manic-Depressive States and the Pre-Genital Levels of the Libido" in *Selected Papers of Karl Abraham M.D.* London: Hogarth Press.
8. Klein, M. 1940. "Mourning and Its Relation to Manic-Depressive States" in *The International Journal of Psycho-Analysis* 21: 125–53.
9. Grinberg, L. 1992. *Guilt and Depression*. New York: Karnac Books.
10. Cf. Lacan, J. 2021. *The Object Relation: The Seminar of Jacques Lacan, Book IV*. Cambridge: Polity.
11. This paragraph reproduces almost verbatim a paragraph from the Introduction of Seminar IV, *The Object Relation* (1956–1957)
12. *A questão do objeto no campo freudiano* [The Question of the Object in the Freudian Field]. Idem 2.

13. This topic is discussed in greater detail in the section "The Pain of Mourning" in this same book.

14. Juan David Nasio remarked in a personal communication that Lacan had the inspiration for the idea of the "object *a*" during a lecture on *Mourning and Melancholia*. Lacan mentioned it in one of his Italian conferences.

15. Shakespeare, W. 2002. "Sonnet XXII," in *The Oxford Shakespeare: The Complete Sonnets and Poems*. Oxford: Oxford University Press

16. We are referring to what Lacan (2006) proposes in his third point of "Remarks on Daniel Lagache's Presentation: "Psychoanalysis and Personality Structure" in Écrits, where he made progress on the formulation of the optical model and proposed 90-degree rotation of the plane mirror that represents the Other, so that the subject can access the place of the ego-ideal, a movement where the illusion of the ideal ego collapses.

BIBLIOGRAPHY

Abraham, K. 1927. "Manic-Depressive States and the Pre-Genital Levels of the Libido" in *Selected Papers of Karl Abraham M.D.* London: Hogarth Press.

Freud, S. 1957a. "Mourning and Melancholia" in *The Standard Edition of the Complete Psychological Works of Sigmund Freud[SE], Vol. XIV*. London: The Hogarth Press and the Institute of Psychoanalysis, 237–58.

Freud, S. 1958. "Totem and Taboo," in *SE, Vol. XIII*, 1–163.

Freud, S. 1959a. "Inhibitions, Symptoms, and Anguish" in *SE, Vol. XX*, 77–177.

Grinberg, L. 1992. *Guilt and Depression*. New York: Karnac Books.

Klein, M. 1940. "Mourning and Its Relation to Manic-Depressive States" in *The International Journal of Psycho-Analysis* 21: 125–53.

Lacan, J. 2006. "Remarks on Daniel Lagache's Presentation: "Psychoanalysis and Personality Structure" in *Écrits: The First Complete Edition in English*. New York: Norton & Co., 543–74.

Lacan, J. 2014. *Anxiety: the Seminar of Jacques Lacan, Book X*. Cambridge: Polity, trans. A.R. Price.

Lacan, J. 2015. *Transference: The Seminar of Jacques Lacan, Book VIII*, Cambridge: Polity.

Lacan, J. 2021. *The Object Relation: The Seminar of Jacques Lacan, Book IV*. Cambridge: Polity.

Shakespeare, W. 2002."Sonnet XXII," in *The Oxford Shakespeare: The Complete Sonnets and Poems*. Oxford: Oxford University Press.

Vidal, E. 1984. "A questão do objeto no campo freudiano" [The Question of the Object in the Freudian Field] in *O objetonateoria e napráticapsicanalítica*. Rio de Janeiro: Ed. Campus.

Chapter 3

Sexuation and Mourning

THE FORMULAS OF SEXUATION

Sexuation and mourning, the title of the present chapter, are both terms that speak about a limit, a finish, about the end of the endless, and that articulate the particular way in which both sexes deal with the immeasurable enjoyment (*jouissance*) that inhabits within. It's an immeasurable enjoyment, but one essentially shaped by the knot function that the unconscious castration complex exerts on the subject.

We'll try to articulate between mourning as a reaction in the face of a loss, that expresses itself through diverse clinical manifestations, and mourning understood as the process of access to subjectivation, or in other words, as in fundamental mourning, a castration procedure that refers to founding moments and establishes the subjective position of the *parlêtre* as its sexed identity.

The sexed subject, to become such, must go through successive losses. These losses are the price to pay to access the language and become the *parlêtre*. The maximum they can bear to surrender is to not be that which completes the Other: to accept the narcissistic affront of not being the phallus of the Other. This fact puts them in condition to take the word and embark on the road of subjectivation, which is not without anguish. This first paradigmatic surrender of abandonment from the maternal womb to submerge oneself in the bath waters of language and traverse through the coordinates of the Oedipus complex is what Lacan proposes be contemplated with the development of the operations of alienation and separation.

We call the detachment bound to the "being" a first renunciation, given that the next one is linked to "having." Having or not having a phallus refers to a sexed positioning that concerns both sexes. It alludes to an active or passive, masculine or feminine, subjective position. In accordance with how the subject relates to the phallus, they will gain access to a sexed identity. The other sex will become what is radically other. It isn't about having a phallus and exhibiting it all the time, as it can be extremely exhausting, nor permanently allying oneself with dissatisfaction, revealing their phallic lack. It's in the formulas of sexuation where that sexed positioning can be read, in accordance with how the lack acted on the subject.

Lacan took up again, in his return to Freud, the order of differences. In fact, he reasserts them, emphasizing their clinical effects. And, despite having all the Women's Liberation Movement against him, he moved forward, trying to specify said differences, better frame the question about the enigma of femininity, and delving into them without confusing them with an imaginary issue of inequality between the sexes.

"The Signification of the Phallus" begins with the affirmation that "the unconscious castration complex functions as a knot" (Lacan 2006, 575). I cite this verbatim because I think it introduces us really well to these formulas. It's possible to see that in 1958, several years before trying to capture sexuality in logical formulas, the idea that Lacan would later sustain was already exhibited in his writings. The very first sentence of that text is, then:

We know that the unconscious castration complex functions as a knot.

1) In the dynamic structuring of symptoms, in the analytical sense of the term, in other words, in the dynamic structuring of what is analyzable in the neuroses, perversions and psychoses.
2) In regulating the development that gives its *ratio* [reason] to this first role: namely, the instating in the subject of an unconscious position [an unconscious sexed position] without which he could not identify with the ideal type of his sex or even answer the needs of his partner in sexual relationships without grave risk, much less appropriately meet the needs of the child who may be produced thereby. (Lacan 2006, 575)

Thus, we said that even if there is not a representation of the sexual tendency, what is present, at an unconscious level, is a position taken in relation to the sexed identity.

Copulation and reproduction are strictly biological concepts. That there be a sexually anatomical difference is a necessary condition to determine the psychic consequences, but it's not enough. The Other, the Other of the language, the Other of the driven demand, the Other that affects the subject from the most obscure part of their unconscious will delineate the coordinates where they will display their sexuality.

Freud spoke about sexuality. Sexuality is in the field of consciousness. With the concept of sexuation, Lacan indicates the unconscious position that affects a subject. That's why the formulas of sexuation that he would display later illustrate the divided field between both tendencies—feminine or masculine—which lay out the position of the subject in relation to the phallus, the primordial signifier with respect to which the sexed position of the human cub is ordered.

What can be seen from giving a quick look at such formulas is that from both fields, feminine and masculine, enjoyment is accessed in a strictly different way. We note that on the feminine side an unfolding occurs, and on the masculine side there is only a unidirectional arrow that points to the target to where the access to sexual satisfaction is directed.

In the Seminar XX, *Encore* (1972–1973), when the sexuation formulas are spoken of, formulas that allude to logic are introduced.

The logic being dealt with is Aristotelian logic, the logic of quantifiers.

What is logic? Why should we resort to formulas to talk about sexuality?

When the mindset centered on logic emerged among the Greek, it was in response to what spread in the middle, which was sophistry. Sophisms are confusing arguments, similar to valid ones, but that have no substance.

Then Aristotle presented the *Organon*, the first work on logic. In it he presented a logic substantiated on a mathematical formulation that touched on something real. He was trying to achieve a mathematical writing that would account for what's real.

Regarding the formulas of sexuation, that reality that Lacan tried to formalize, to give a mathematical writing, entailed enjoyment. I would add that they try to logically write out the mode in which the feminine and masculine deal with enjoyment. In this line of argument, it would be needless to say that a man can have a feminine way to experience enjoyment, and a woman could

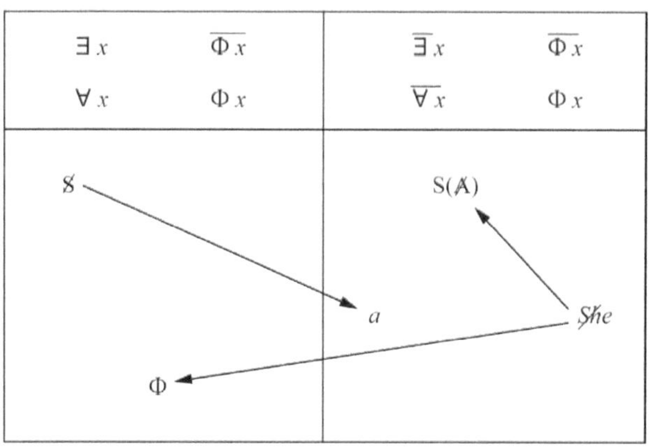

Figure 3.1 Graph I, Formulas of Sexuation, Seminar XX, Encore (1972–1973). *Source:* Created by the author.

experience enjoyment in a masculine way, and this is susceptible to the infinitely nuanced combinations that can be made.

A logical formula is a mathematical expression, and as such it allows for several variations; the only condition it presents is that a true value, and not a false one, must be maintained between its propositions.

In Freudian teachings, especially in the texts that allude to the differences established in boys and girls as a consequence of the dissolution of the Oedipus complex, and also in those covering female sexuality, that distinction in the encounter with the drive for satisfaction is described and analyzed extensively. Formulas of sexuation provide a logical support to the modes of the satisfaction drive for the feminine and masculine, beyond the Oedipal drama and the dichotomy of gender division.

These formulas speak about mortals, about subjects. On the left side are going to be those who say that they are men, and on the right side will be those who say that they are women.

Let's stop for a moment in the female side of the diagram, that for the moment is the one that interests us for moving forward in the relationship between the woman and the phallus, with the lack and the notion of unfolding. We emphasize the part of the formula that says—not all x, Φ of x. This formulation corresponds to the *La* matheme. Meanwhile, on the male side, the universal quantifier which is "for all" comprises men, the universe of men and says, "All x, anyone that calls himself a man is affected by the phallic function." On the female side it slips into "not all women are affected by the phallic signifier."

A part of her is related to the phallus, and by unfolding, the rest is related to the signifier of the lack in the Other. It's an entry point to another enjoyment, a feminine enjoyment, whose condition is to subtract herself from having all phallic enjoyment. It's a subtraction that allows the unfolding of the arrow on the female side of the table.

This understanding of the formulas of sexuation allows for a linkage with the Freudian texts, and it also helps to detect in what parts Lacan advances with respect of Freud, on the question of femininity.

Let us turn to Freud. He says in the conference on *Female Sexuality*, that for woman, the sinking of the Oedipus complex is not as such. She finds a safe haven in loving the father. Disillusioned by the mother, she changes the object. She turns to the father and also changes the zone, from the clitoris to the vagina, from the mother to the father. The disillusionment confines her to the place of someone that's deprived (in the sense of lacking a penis as an organ), and it's from there that she goes to look for it in the father.

Following the Freudian path, in *On Transformations of Instinct as Exemplified in Anal Erotism* (1917), Freud puts penis-baby-gift-feces on the same level. He highlights that, for the childish mind of the little girl, the desire that has priority is that of having "the little one[*das Kleine*]" (Freud 1955b, 128) with an equivalence prevailing between the elements of the series, not having influenced the phallic primacy yet. This logic of equivalences between heterogeneous variables rules in the anal phase. It's a phase in which the object oscillates between expulsion and retention, without having operated the phallic phase and the castration complex yet. The sexual differences don't influence the dynamics of the amorous crossroads yet.

The position of the girl with regards to the boy, that demands the father, isn't a position from the place of a woman, but a position from a place from which she aspires to retain him as the phallic object that redeems her lack of it.

In clinical cases, it's not uncommon to find women that have children in this position. They have an attitude of possessing them, without having in consideration that in "their boy" there's emerging a subject that is absolutely singular.[1] Assuming this absolutely egoistic relationship toward them can happen with their own children, or even with their grandchildren.

It was evident in the complaint of a grandmother that, while griping about her son not going to her house to visit, and, in that way, preventing her from seeing her grandson, she exclaimed, "I want to enjoy having the baby around. I lose the chance to enjoy having a grandson if I don't see him—and she added, with a tinge of paranoia—everyone gets to enjoy him more than me." There was no consideration at all about what was happening to the boy, if he wanted to see her, how much did he enjoy being around her, what could she do to be closer to her grandson.

That's not the mother's position. If one of the attributes of motherhood is abnegation, whose definition is "renouncing oneself," we could deduce that being a mother involves renouncing, to stop enjoying that transitory completeness that pregnancy and the first moments of child-rearing grant.

From the Difference of the Inscription to the Inscription of the Difference

Let's try reading a paragraph from Seminar XX, *Encore* (1972–1973), extracted from the class on February 13, 1973, which presented difficulties in its translation. Thus, it has been interpreted in several ways. This is why I will provide my own translation and interpretation. It's an essential paragraph for the comprehension of the formulas and for approaching the notion of supplementary enjoyment, also known as the enjoyment of the Other or feminine enjoyment. It reads as follows:

> It is false that there is another. That won't stop me from playing once more on the equivocation based on *faux* (false), by saying that it shouldn't (*faux-drait*)

> be/could never fail to be/could never fail to be/couldn't be false that it is that one. Suppose that there is another—but there isn't. And, simultaneously, it is not because there isn't—and because it is on this that "it shouldn't be/could be never fail" depend—that the cleaver falls any the less on the jouissance with which we began. The one has (*faut*) to be, failing (*faute de*)—you should understand that as guilt—failing the other that is not. (Lacan 1999, 60)

It's an obscure phrase. It speaks about enjoyment. It speaks about the cleaver that falls on the enjoyment with which we began. Did the controversy revolve around which enjoyment we began with, which enjoyment he refers to, the enjoyment of the Other or the phallic enjoyment?

In our reading, we accompany this paragraph with another one from a later class that says,

> That is nevertheless what is written on the blackboard with the arrow that begins from ~~Woman~~. ~~Woman~~ cannot be said (*se dire*). Nothing can be said of woman. Woman has a relation with S(Ⱥ), and it is already in that respect that she is doubled, that she is not-whole, since she can also have a relation with Φ. (Lacan 1999, 81)

We understand that, in this context, the enjoyment with which "we begin" refers to the phallic enjoyment, whose partition promotes the doubling, or unfolding, to which he then alludes to, and which opens up her enjoyment to run aground in another place, the one destined to be the place where the Other lacks a signifier, a space for the display of another writing of sublimatory enjoyment.

The cleaver falls on the phallic enjoyment to produce this unfolding and to have one part run aground in the phallic enjoyment and the other part in another enjoyment, in the lack of a signifier in the Other. The lack of a signifier in the Other implies a certain knowledge that the subject has attained about the Other, knowing that they lack a signifier, which enables the subject to inscribe themselves with their letters, the ones that were passed on to them, but rearranging them according to their own desire. That relationship with the lack of the Other calls for a supplementary enjoyment, which in the field of culture is linked to the written letter as a paradigmatic unit of the marks of civilization, in the bond between the members of a community.

We arrived up to this point to make the conjecture that, for the cleaver to split the enjoyment with which we begin, the phallic enjoyment, some transformation should be produced within the aforementioned symbolic equation, in which the variables are presented as equivalents, meaning: penis=boy=feces=gift.

The transformation that we're speaking of would then consist in the boy taking the place of a son, accessing a different place, not one of an indistinct variable in the series of transmutations.

The more effectively the castration was carried out, the higher the probability that the transformation, the transition from being in the place of the boy, "the little one," to the place of the son, is brought to fruition; thus, there is the access for the woman to an enjoyment beyond the phallic. When the anal phase comes first, the boy is trapped in a relationship of retention–expulsion. The son, phantasmatically, embodies the phallicity in the woman. Being the all-mother, a phallic mother, subjects her, on occasion, to conversive symptoms in her body, intimately related to the moments of subjective growth of her children.[2]

I think it's significant that when Lacan introduces that other enjoyment, he ties it to the term "guilt"—see the paragraph translated above. It would appear that it concerns the guilt that tarnishes the maternal–filial relationship when it's immersed completely in the phallic enjoyment. Thus, frequently, faced with even the most minimum separation or minute malaise from the child, relentless self-accusations are triggered within the mother, and a guilt seizes her, the maximum imaginarized expression of enjoyment.

The transformation would consist of the boy being given a different place, not one of an indistinct variable in the series of transmutations, but becoming a singular term with whom there is no suitable relationship possible: a son, a gift, or, if you will, a gift for the culture.

This would effectuate a transition between the desires of the boy, originally essential for investing libidinally in the *infans*, to what we could call the renunciation of the boy. To re-enunciate the absence where the child comes and plugs it up. I think that this is the link that would allow finding a different exit, a singular one, beyond that safe haven—the love for the son is a "rerun" of the love for the father in the economics of femininity—that sometimes imprisons her.

With this Freud is categorical: in the woman there is no burial of the Oedipus complex. She finds a safe haven in her love for the father. It seems that what she is always unknowledgeable of is how imprisoned she remains to the haven that saved her.

In the formulas of sexuation, we can find the ways that those who call themselves male or female relate to enjoyment, in accordance to a modality that expresses that there isn't a sexual relationship,[3] given that between man and woman, as is affirmed by the founder of psychoanalysis, "There are consequences . . . of the distinction." Differences that transcend the real of the sexually anatomical so that differences, sometimes tenuous and at other times relevant, can transpire in all the planes of its manifestations.[4]

The female side seems to have, in its specificity, a privileged way of connecting with the lack that determines a particular modality of being in touch with enjoyment, a singular way of satisfaction of their drive. We call this way, according to the developments proposed in the sexuation formulas, an *unfolded* way. This is how the feminine side, as far as the modality of enjoyment goes, is bound to the way in which a subject builds an argument or phantasmatic position with regards to the phallic primacy, but also beyond it. The feminine part attached to another enjoyment, a sublimatory enjoyment that orders a script, would be the patrimony of every *parlêtre*, regardless of the sex that they carry.

The operations of alienation and separation propose two logical moments to think about the constitution of subjectivity. Such operations are not far removed from the constitution of the sexed identity. In other words, we propose that the sexed positions and the differences that concern them are the result of how the fundamental lack, the fecund lack, the founding castration is processed. Thus, the feminine or virile position denounces a particular relationship regarding the lack. This will impact the distinct ways that those who consider themselves a man or woman will react in the face of the loss of the loved object.

Our question revolves around identifying what the different ways of reacting in the face of losses consist of, according to those who identify themselves as a man or woman.

Paraphrasing the well-known article by Freud, *Some Psychical Consequences of the Anatomical Distinction between the Sexes*, we propose reducing it to its core and affirming that there are consequences of the distinction, particularly in the way they manage losses (Freud 1961a).[5]

Said consequences can be pondered in light of the neologism introduced by Lacan. To talk about sexuality he invents the "formulas of sexuation."

I understand that introducing a neologism to speak about sexuality declares that the topic of the sexed identity extensively transcends the issue of feminine or masculine gender. To speak about sexuation and introduce mathematical formulas suggest a logic that subverts the establishment of gender stereotypes.

Continuing with the aforementioned developments, thinking that there are "consequences of the distinction" links those differences to the effects of castration and the Oedipus complex.

At this point I'm going to briefly go through what Freud places as the dissolution: the burial of the Oedipus complex, which isn't just a simple repression.

In men, the completion of the Oedipus complex has to do with the threat of castration. The renunciation occurs to not succumb to a feminine position. If he identifies himself with the father, taking the object of the father, that is, the mother, there's a risk of losing the organ. If he identifies himself with the mother, on the other hand, he also pays the price of feminization. The threat spreads across the reality of losing it or not.

Without a doubt, for women the threat comes down different lanes. If she doesn't have anything in the real, then there is nothing to lose. The panic doesn't spread to preserve any organ, so the only thing that's left is to try and attain it.

In this way, women don't have that same burial. There is no dissolution of the Oedipus complex. On the contrary, its culmination prompts a search that leads her to the father. Through that prompt she finds in her love for the father a place to fasten herself.

For women, the Oedipus complex isn't buried. It escapes the demolition given that she finds a safe haven in her love for the father. Disillusioned by the mother, she changes her object and moves toward the father. In her course of action she'll also change the zone, from the clitoris to the vagina. Conspicuously, it's a cavity that encloses the access to the sexual enjoyment. Traveling from one cavity to another, the woman will later find in the womb another cavity which will become her interest. It's the cavity of the body prepared to care for the child [*das Kleine*]. The boy assumes the place of an imaginary headquarters for the achievement of a yearned completeness in the woman. It's delayed materialization of a demand originally directed toward the father.

Expecting a boy to fill such cavities, the woman, through the *infans*, will be stuck in that feminine impasse. I say that feminine impasse because, when reading Freudian texts, if you try to think about the enigma of femininity, what you will find are three possible outcomes, each one of them encountering a limit.

What are those three paths indicated by Freud?

First, sexual inhibition and repression, with its inevitable resurgence in hysteric symptoms.

Second, the masculinity complex. Identifying herself with her father and staying in that virilized position.

The third outcome goes through the son. Through motherhood, she fulfills her feminine identity.

Nevertheless, clinical studies frequently teach us that motherhood, more than the fulfillment of femininity, is a limit, a shortcut that obstructs the wide display of the issue of her desire as a woman.

Motherhood and femininity are disjointed notions. They don't overlap. Paradoxically, on different occasions, the son serves to stop up symptoms, sustain the mystery of femininity, tolerate certain deviations of identity or accept an unfolding in how she deals with enjoyment. They follow suit with the feminine condition.

Recapping, the subjectivation of the human offspring carries traces of its position with respect to the phallus: having it or not is the milepost.

Nevertheless, the preliminary condition is the discovery of what is not. Not being it requires two operations that are conjoined in the domain of the Other: alienation and separation. Both operations of the subjective constitution carve out the way in which the subject will wield their relationship with the constituted lack.

Regarding these functions, Lacan proposes in his Seminar XI, *The Four Fundamental Concepts of Psychoanalysis* (1964) to pose them in terms of the coating of two absences. The first one has to do with this function of alienation, which implies that the subject constitute themselves in the place of the Other, the signifier. They stay right there, almost disappearing under the meaning that the Other attributes to them.

The second absence signifies itself retroactively in a new way, given that it's proposed as a previous absence, previous to that first one. It's the instituted lack because they are a sexed being that's submissive to death. Being subdued to the generational sequence makes the subject face death. It pushes them to decide to go after meaning in what is becoming of their destiny, expropriating it by being.

Alienation and separation are the names that were used by Lacan to express the access to subjectivation. It's from these functions that the subject is thrown into the Oedipal dynamics, into the vicissitudes of castration.

Thus, we affirm that the threat of castration falls differently on the subject, depending on whether they are said to be a boy or a girl. With that we understand that the psychical consequences transcend the anatomical sexual distinction.

It's on the biological plane, under the aegis of the anatomical sexual distinction, that the copulation between the two different sexes is spoken about. The definition of the term "copulation" that María Moliner's dictionary gives is, "A complete union of the gametes in the protozoa, a union between the male and female of higher animals for fertilization."[6] We stress that copulation is only on the biological plane. On the plane of the subject there is alienation and separation.

The function of reproduction, which is founded in the sexual tendency (understanding this, by which the distinction is made between what's feminine and masculine), is only displayed on the biological plane; there is no preconceived representation in the psyche.[7]

It's only on the biological plane and in the act of reproduction where it becomes reality that "anatomy is destiny."

In the psyche, nothing exists that the subject can use to orient themselves as being a male or female. So, we come back to the question, how are there psychical consequences of the anatomical distinction between sexes? If Lacan affirmed that there isn't anything in the psyche that makes someone able to call themselves a female or male, how do we consider the psychical consequences that Freud spoke about?

Lacan resolved such a crossroads by appealing to theoretical rigor, and thus deduced that, in the psyche, the anatomical sexual difference presents itself through equivalences. Not with a representation, but with equivalents that are far from representing it exhaustively.

What are these equivalents? Activity and passivity. These are the polarizations that the psyche adopts to speak about the anatomical sexual difference. At this point, he leans on what Freud would mention on several occasions.

It's in *Analysis Terminable and Interminable* (1937) where Freud seems to loosen those radical postures about passivity and activity for each one of the sexes, and he stresses once again the prevalence of the differences that show up at the end of an analysis for a man or woman. He says that for the woman, it'd be having to abandon or getting through the penis envy. We could interpret, using this formulation, that she shouldn't find in her allotted passivity, or lack of a penis, the point of outburst that makes her symptomatically hoist herself up permanently as a phallus.

For the man, the end of the analysis would consist in straddling that hostile position with his male peers, tolerating on occasion a passive posture regarding the others of his same sex.

For Lacan, the polarity of the male and female being manifests itself in the psyche only by equivalents of each sexual tendency. In German this is called *Trieb*. Tracking down the meaning of the German term *Trieb*, its translation to English can't be reduced to just drive. The translation given by the dictionary of its verbal form is to stimulate, to incite. That is why the concept of drive is masculine: because it's tied to the initiative of stimulating. This position of activity is equivalent to the masculine sexual tendency. For the feminine sexual tendency, what corresponds is an inciting—a *Trieb*—that on the outside takes on the appearance of passivity.

It's the word of the Other, the letter of the Other, that gives the subject an argument for inscribing something—of that which doesn't cease to not be registered—in the psyche as active or passive. From there they will receive the resources that will allow them to advance in the erotic game with their *partenaire*.

Mourning operating in the subject is also mourning for the other sex, a process that involves expansion by penetrating the virtues of the sex that inhabits it, without vying aggressively with the opposite sex.

Regarding losses of loved ones, that marked distinction in relation to the lack of both sexes has repercussions concerning how they face them. From there it can be seen the completely different ways in which women in communities have expressed mourning for their men. The Greek left eloquent samples of the stance that their women adopted in those circumstances.

Demanding a Child of the Father: Their Stumbles

We can say that most of the times women arrive for analysis with an impeded access to a pleasant position of their feminine condition. They frequently come in, sick, suffering, demanding. Some of them have children and some do not. Nevertheless, in both cases it's unavoidable that the issue of a child emerge during their analysis, to then have to get to some kind of renouncement. Renouncing a child in what is inherently childlike of them, the *das Kleine*, will open up their access to the other enjoyment, different from the phallic one. An enjoyment bound irrevocably to a loss, to mourning, that makes the absence available, so as to raise the object to the quality of the thing.

Dalia is a woman that went for consultation almost at the age limit of her biological fertility, around her forties. In the first few interviews, she told how in a previous consultation, and a pretty recent one at that, the central topic was about whether or not she wanted to have a child with her partner. When she got pregnant, a few weeks afterward she started to feel that the transformation of her body was unbearable. She couldn't tolerate even thinking about "that thing that was growing inside." So she had an abortion without talking about it with her partner, with whom she had recently celebrated the news of her pregnancy. She made no comment about it, and, in a clear exhibition of acting out, she decided to abandon what was beginning to appear to be an ongoing analysis.

This wasn't her first abortion, but before she had never remained so anguished and depressed afterward. In addition, her drinking habits returned. She would stay locked up in her home drinking for days, missing her daily activities.

While in her professional life she had managed to set up something that sustained her and allowed her to carry out activities that she liked, her affective life was characterized by labile and unsteady relationships.

In recent times, what was peculiar was that she was going out with men that were much younger than her, that she dubbed "insignificants." She subjected herself to a variety of mistreatments on their part.

Her actual partner Juan was an alcoholic, abused drugs, and is an HIV carrier. She said that she tried to make him change almost with a motherly dedication.

Regarding her family, she mentioned that the relationship she had with her mother and sister was very distant, even more distant ever since her sister got married and took their mother to live with her in a different place. "I always felt uncomfortable around them, like excluded." Her father had passed away two years ago. He had for many years maintained an affair with one of her mother's older sisters. Her mother was taken by surprise upon finding them kissing in her own house. She also remembered instances when her father brought a woman to dinner that nobody knew, while making the excuse that she helped him at the newspaper stand.

In her teenage years she was a rebel, fighting constantly with her sister. She had intercourse for the first time at fifteen, and when her parents found out, which was because her mother found the diary where she had written about it, a scandal broke out that involved a beating and grounding.

She considered herself her father's favorite over her sister, in spite of the fact that when she turned eighteen, with different excuses lined up for the family needing to move to a smaller apartment, he asked her to move into a boarding house.

A revealing memory: At the Retiro Station, she believed she was around four or five years old, her father sat her down to reserve both seats while he went to buy train tickets. There were a lot of people. "I started to panic," she said.

Her father had passed away two years prior. She kept the clothes that belonged to him in her house, inside the closets. It was a complaint she had for a while, not having enough space for his stuff. It was another way of saving him the seat. She wore those clothes, especially an overcoat that she loved to wear.

On one occasion—she took the overcoat off of the hanger she always had it on and, without looking at it, put it on the carpet, on the floor, and said, "It can stay over there."

In the same session she spoke about Juan and her decision to end the relationship she had with him. It was after an incident where he got drunk and started being violent at a gathering with friends. They had already separated and gotten together again various times during their tumultuous relationship, but this time she said, "I choose to not have him around." What can be heard, and what she herself professes can be heard is, "That the child not be around." (TN: There is a wordplay here where the Spanish for I choose sounds like son or child.) It's a way to express the place granted to that *partenaire* in the relationship.

This material seems extremely interesting to me for thinking about the desire of a woman to have a child as a demand directed toward the father first and then a man. Considering this case was about a woman without children, who went through serious vicissitudes related to that, this proves to be a paradigmatic clinical excerpt for thinking about the consequences incurred on the desire of the maternal function when, due to serious shortcomings in the paternal function, that demand doesn't get transferred to another man, and the demand toward the father perseveres.

If the place of a daughter in relation to her father has not been abandoned, if her mourning for her father has not been processed, it's difficult for the woman to access a place where she can display her traits, even motherhood.

ANNA O. TURNED ONE HUNDRED YEARS OLD

More than a hundred years have passed since Sigmund Freud convinced Josef Breuer to include a section dedicated to the medical history of Bertha Pappenheim, written about under the pseudonym Anna O., in the publication of *Studies on Hysteria* (1893–1995).

Anna O. was a clinical case that, thirteen years prior, Breuer had referred to Freud, drawing his attention to the cathartic method as the means to resolving the hysterical conversion symptoms.

What this renowned doctor at the end of the century in Vienna transmitted to the young Sigmund on November 18, 1882, was a clinic experience that he had been led to upon being compelled to study the symptoms of a twenty-one-year-old woman who turned out to be a friend of Martha Bernays, Freud's fiancée.

The Medical History

Let us briefly remember what symptoms afflicted Anna when she had the consultation with Breuer. She had a chronic cough, the doctor described her as typically being anxious, she was markedly exhausted in the afternoon, she had strabismus, headaches, paralysis, and numbness in various parts (neck muscles, upper right and lower limbs). She spent most of the day in an absent state of mind, where she was detached and disconnected from the circumstances that surrounded her.

After starting the treatment, other alterations appeared, such as a growing disorganization in the functionality of language that advanced to the point where she couldn't speak in German, her mother tongue. She expressed herself in English, French, or Italian. She also suffered from anguish attacks. On some occasions they were accompanied by elemental phenomena such as visual hallucinations of black snakes that approached the bedside of her sick father, sometimes extending from her fingers.

She rejected food, showing symptoms of anorexia, and also water, even though she was extremely thirsty. On some occasions she showed suicidal intent, which made it inadvisable for her to live on the third floor, so her family moved to a house in the countryside of Vienna.

It was during this period of time of the treatment when the so-called second state of consciousness, or hypnoid state, or absences, or as she called it, her private theater, became more intense.

It consisted of a regression to a time of the past, to the point where she would fictitiously reproduce day by day what she had experienced exactly a year before, the previous winter. Breuer clarified that through the private diary of Anna's mother, it was easy to corroborate the accuracy of such memories.

It is worth mentioning that Anna's sickness coincided with when her father became bedridden. He had become seriously ill in July of 1880 from a subpleural abscess caused by tuberculosis that led him to his death in April of 1881. The patient, who had been at his bedside from the beginning of his illness, assisting him day and night, had to step away from those duties because of the worsening of her own state of health. Moreover, she was forbidden from going to see him during the last two months prior to his death, and they even withheld the news of his death for a few days, though she had already started to suspect it.

Josef Breuer treated her from December of 1880 until June of 1882. Ernest Jones recalled that by then, far from being cured, the patient developed a pseudocyesis, that is, a false pregnancy. The culmination of the fantasized pregnancy during the treatment was when a huge scene was made, almost a scene about the scene of analysis, where the patient started to cry out "Dr. Breuer's baby is coming," to which he responded by running away in a cold sweat. She was then hospitalized for a few months in a clinic outside Vienna.

Years later Freud points out that Breuer had his hands on the "master key," but he didn't know how to use it. He was referring to transference, that key concept of psychoanalysis that its creator knew how to take into account from the early stages as a tool in the treatment.

Thus far, that's the florid hysteria of Anna O., conversive, hallucinatory, theatrical, enigmatic, maddening almost to the limit of how dangerous it can be for those who dared to try something different, since the usual practice was to lump her together with the demonized or mentally degenerate. Beyond the symptoms, nevertheless, the so often denigrated and belittled hysteria undeniably proposes, both at the origins of psychoanalysis and still today, a modality of speech that interrogates and questions the established wisdom.

The way that hysteria pierces through the established discourses of its time, not without making use of them, promotes something in the order of invention. Anna created terms in English such as "talking cure" and "chimney sweeping" to talk about the value of catharsis, related to being cured by the word.

The concept of catharsis was studied at that time in cultural halls of Vienna at the end of the century. Indeed, a book by Jacob Bernays (the uncle of Freud's future wife) had just been published about the Aristotelian notion of the term *catharsis*, stemming from the Greek tragedy. "Time missing" was another term created by Anna to designate her "absences" when being absent from the world that surrounded her and joyfully locked up in her "private theatre," her dreams or fantasies.

Who Was Bertha Pappenheim?

She belonged to a respected family from a very close off orthodox Jewish circle. Her grandfather was an important figure in the Pressburg ghetto. Her father, Siegmund Pappenheim, was a wealthy merchant from Vienna that had founded a synagogue.

Bertha was the middle sister in between a sister that was ten years older than her, who passed away when she was a teenager, and a little brother, who was one year younger, that became a distinguished lawyer, open to the ideas of modernity and with what was probably the library in Europe with the most books about socialism.

She spent her youth and teenage years with that family, where, at the time, the prerogative for girls was to take piano lessons, make crafts, and to attend tea parties where they were to display good manners and a refined taste. This is the Viennese period where Anna found herself, which we know about due to the story of her illness covered by Breuer.

A short time after her father's death in 1882, the family moved to Frankfurt, where Bertha started to unfurl an intense interest in social work, first in the disgraced and decadent Judengasse ghetto. In 1895, she was appointed director of the Jewish orphanage for girls. Later, she founded different institutions for the care of poor children and marginalized young women, the unprotected minorities in the impoverished Europe of the beginning of the century.

She also dedicated herself to the translation of several texts of Jewish tradition from Yiddish to German. She wrote a collection of stories, plays, poems, and aphorisms. She issued a manifesto or open letter denouncing the precarious lifestyle of the Jews in Galicia. She also founded a newspaper, where she was laureated the day she died by several intellectuals of the time that made collaborations with her, among them Martin Buber.

In 1954, there was a stamp issued in East Germany with a picture of Bertha Pappenheim in the series "Benefactors of Mankind."

Decidedly, in this second stage of her life in Frankfurt, Bertha became—and I do not use this term naively—as the documents of the time testify, a pioneer of welfare work in Central Europe for the underprivileged and disadvantaged minorities.

She put her name on the list of those who were considered illustrious members of society, in a time where restlessness, the decline of ideals, economic crisis, and the increase of racial discrimination reigned.

The question that emerges, then, has to do with the essence of hysteria: Does there exist any relationship between conversive hysteria and the feminine, more precisely, that supplementary enjoyment that characterizes the feminine position? Could it be possible to access femininity without going beyond that disposition of the woman's body for conversion?

I suggest that Anna's medical history and Bertha's biography give privileged material for thinking about that thin littoral that divides the waters between hysteria and femininity.

After the revelations of Jones about Breuer and Anna, the majority of the written production that I had access to revolved around the inadvertent romantic transference of the patient with her doctor, which culminated in a dramatization of the pains of that hysterical, conversive, and camouflaged birth.

I do not intend to stop this time with the transferential vicissitudes that affected the treatment. Instead, I propose to reread, based on the developments of Seminar XX, *Encore* (1972–1973) by Lacan, the life of the protagonist of the first case of psychoanalysis, the origins.

Bertha Pappenheim, both in her medical history of conversion hysteria and her biography, in which she becomes the founder and pioneer of movements of welfare work, offers an appropriate text to offer some questions about the discourse of hysterical women with regards to the subjectivity of the time and its close relationship with the creative channel of femininity.

From Procreation to Creation: The Unfolding of Enjoyment

I will start from the premise that Seminar XX[8] is an inflection point in theoretical thinking about the feminine, particularly in how it deals with enjoyment, where what is particular is the unfolding.

I will quote from the class on March 13, 1973: "Nothing can be said of woman. Woman has a relation with $S(\not{A})$, and it is already in that respect that she is doubled, that she is not-whole, since she can also have a relation with Φ."

We could say that said unfolding, which implies what in the formulas is shown by a bifurcation of the arrows that depart from the ~~*Woman (She)*~~, ready her for a treatment of enjoyment where its goals of anchorage are diversified.

A woman, the host of a body deprived from an enjoyment circumscribed to an organ, like her partner, remains hysteric, persevering in her demand toward her father, granting him a certain knowledge, loving him. In conversion, it's a body that subverts its own anatomy and leaves her anchored to the phallic enjoyment, unable to navigate such an unfolding.

Nevertheless, it's hysteria, and the medical history of Anna O. illustrates it, what led to thinking about that unfolded capacity which is the driving force behind hysterical women. Double consciousness or dissociative identity disorder is a psychic split to denominate her absentmindedness or hypnoid state; it's the same thing that during the Middle Ages was attributed to being possessed by the Devil himself during the attack.

Can we adjudicate to this conversive property of the female body the capacity of bestowing the feminine with that unfolded treatment of enjoyment? Or posed in a different way, is it this conversive polymorphism, so peculiar to the female body, that opens up the channels for multifaceted, creative production?

Thereby, when the renouncement of the phallic takes place, or what would the same thing, that to renounce is to re-enounce the lack, the bifurcation of the arrow is made possible, where the sublimatory capacity, the direction toward the signifier of the lack in the Other, is one of the destinations for satisfaction. Beyond the phallus, beyond the demand directed at the father, is where the work of mourning is brought about, where the loss passively withstood is actively processed as a lack. When this hard work operates once more, which conduces her to lose what she doesn't have, the woman accesses that unfolding that also crosses her out. It sets her as not-whole and makes her experience enjoyment in her most remote zones, not just in her anatomical body, but in an interwoven body, where the real, symbolic, and imaginary are knotted together.

As symptomatic as the social activity of Bertha Pappenheim can be judged with regards to the protection of deprived children and young, helpless women, often times *bait* for exportation in the "white-slave trade," as is was then called, it creates a quite different order than the conversive suffering of hysteria dictates.

Linked with what we have been discussing, I would like to take a moment at the completion point of the treatment. The conclusion of this analysis, that

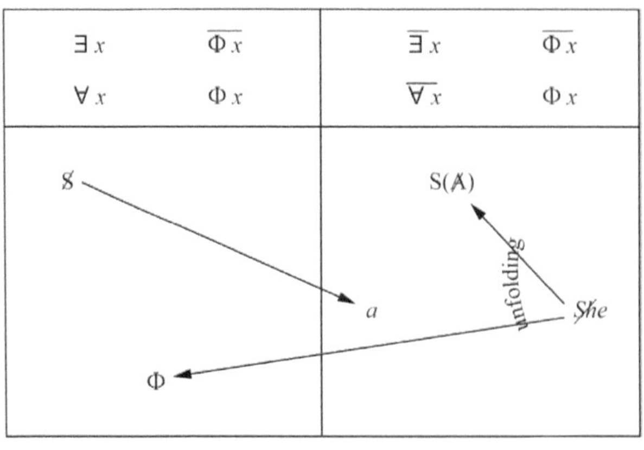

Figure 3.2 Graph II, Formulas of Sexuation, Seminar XX, Encore (1972–1973). *Source:* Created by the author.

was the pseudocyesis of Anna, which came after Breuer's announcement of his next departure due to an extended trip he'd take.

While the extreme distinction between a pregnancy and a pseudopregnancy or conversive pregnancy certainly has its place, I think that considering seriously the place that pregnancy occupies for a woman with regards to her body allows us to grasp some questions.

There are multiple references that theory and praxis offer in order to illustrate the substituted phallic place that a boy means for his mother.

However, little can be found that advances that knowledge with regards to pregnancy, that transformation of the female body that in its deformation lends itself to carry a child.

In fact, with her body's pregnancy, the woman makes public what belongs to the most private sphere. She takes the evidence out for a walk that testifies to the intimacy of her sexual act.

In the first class of the Seminar X, *Anxiety* (1962–1963), Lacan proposes a matrix with axes, taking anguish as their pivot, where the horizontal axis moves with respect to difficulty, and the vertical axis moves with respect to movement. It's a matrix that allows us to take note of inhibition, symptoms, and anguish in the clinical case.

In the first line of cells, along the difficulty axis he first places *inhibition*. He defines it as the symptom that has been put in the museum; the subject does not know it. Afterward he puts *impediment*, from the Latin *impedicare*, being caught in a trap, the actual anxious face of the symptom. For the third term, and almost surprisingly, we find the term *embarrassment*. We can read from the seminar:

> Embarrassment is quite precisely the subject S decked out with the bar. . . . When you don't know what to do with yourself anymore, you look for something behind which to shield yourself. The experience of the bar is precisely what's at issue. If I've been well informed, this bar assumes more than one form . . . in Spanish, the *embarazada*, she who is embarrassed, designates a pregnant woman. . . . [The first row] ends up at this slight form of anguish called embarrassment. (Lacan 2014, 11)

In the last meeting of the seminar, where he replaced the terms of said matrix with other equivalents, instead of embarrassment he put the "concept of anguish," alluding to the terminology of Sören Kierkegaard, where said concept arose at the limit of a meditation.

The philosopher says that women have more of an anxious relationship regarding desire than men. He said it like this,

> The expression of the difference is that anguish is more reflected in Eve than in Adam. This is because the woman is more sensuous than the man. Here of

> course it is not a matter of an empirical state, or of an average number, but of the dissimilarity in the synthesis. . . . Already here the investigation has seen that the proportion of sensuousness corresponds to that of anguish. (Kierkegaard 2014, 78)

Probably taking from these same ideas Lacan said some years earlier, in his writing *The Signification of the Phallus* (1958), that the woman tolerates frigidity better than the *Verdrängung* inherent in desire, while with the man the inverse is true regarding impotence.

If anguish is that untied reality, pregnancy comes with tape to tie up that untethered affection that overflows.

Anna's conversive pregnancy proclaimed a truth that was already starting to make Mrs. Breuer uncomfortable. Anna, with her falsely impregnated body, became a threat that would make a love story, though unconsummated, go public. A story that also appears to have had consequences on the private life of the renowned doctor from Vienna.

The female body, with its particular way of orienting itself with regards to the phallus, keeps that conversive capacity that, upon having passed through it, results in a beyond that opens up channels for the production of knowledge. Placing the object that induces the hysterical woman in the place of truth, as is stated by the discourse that characterizes her, fosters a social bond in which knowledge is produced.

Frequently, it's making a Master consistent, an S1 in the place of the Other, that puts the device in motion that produces a particular knowledge in the subject. That is how the hysterical women at the end of the nineteenth century gave rise to the creation of psychoanalysis. In the transferential device, it's through the road of the subject's assumed knowledge that distinguishes from an Other carrier of an absolute knowledge, where the lack will be carved out, in the Other and in the subject, which allows for surprising and fertile findings for the deployment or unfolding of femininity.

We had started the rereading of the first psychoanalysis case based off of the formulations in Seminar XX, *Encore* (1972–1973). Upon finishing these reflections, we cautioned that it was also a retrospective look at the enigma of femininity from the end of the twentieth century.

Beyond the polymorphism that conversion hysteria presented in central Europe at the end of the century, which was quite tied to the limited roles assigned to women in society, and after all the feminist confusions that, flying under the flag of gender equality, denied what was essential of the difference, that is, the impossibility of sexual relationships. Today hysteria, with its discourse that promotes a certain knowledge, brings about new clues for thinking about femininity and that supplementary enjoyment that characterizes it.

I do not think it necessary to judge what Breuer's treatment brought to Anna. Did it cure her? Did it make her worse? Did he get her pregnant? On the other hand, we can say without any doubt that Bertha Pappenheim knew about the reach that words in transference can have: to stir, to stir what is real.

Femininity and Its Mysteries

In "Cancionero y romancero de ausencias" (Songbook and Balladbook of Absence), a posthumous book of Miguel Hernández, the Spanish poet writes:

Except for your womb, all is confused,
except for your womb, all insecure,
everything last, dust without a world.
Except for your womb, all is dark,
except for your clear and deep womb. (Hernández 1985, 61)[9]

With these letters the poet recites what is women's most substantive property, the faculty that preserves her body for procreating a child, for motherhood.[10] This is neither a mystery, nor is it what makes up the enigma of femininity.

However, the female body, historically, has been the headquarters of the unknown for institutions of knowledge. The clinical science that we are interested in originated as an offer to listen to those suffering bodies.

In spite of the fact that hysteria and femininity sometimes seem to be linked by a certain complicity that intertwines them, during an analysis the distinction that flows out from one to another will become apparent.

On the path from hysteria to femininity, there will appear symptoms, complaints, pains, overwhelming or narcissistically absent mothers, idealized or impotent fathers, and a enjoyment that on occasion places itself in a privileged spot—the one assigned to a son—for its phallic version. The female body—all mother—demands another birth, which is carried out during the hour of the analysis. It's an intervention carried out in the real that, through the presence of the analyst, exerts a subtraction of said enjoyment.

There are several questions about the topic of the eternal feminine. What does a woman want? Where do women have enjoyment? How do they experience enjoyment?

Sometimes they're answered far too quickly with an oversimplification that undermines them. They are questions which too quickly lead to the common ground of the insatiable dissatisfaction typical of the feminine brew.

When Freud, in the beginning of his research, introduced himself to the suffering of his hysterical patients, he discovered a property that lay within those bodies. He called it the capacity for conversion. Bodies that shook convulsively, were paralyzed, became numb, that vomited or starved themselves—anorexic—, that sometimes had their voices affected by dysphonia or muteness, others that were besieged by hallucinations or even . . . that mysteriously became pregnant.

The text where the word conversion is first mentioned is from 1894—*Neuro-Psychosis of Defense*. There, opposing Janet and Breuer, who characterized hysteria as the dissociation of consciousness and hypnoid states, he distinguishes the *capacity for conversion* as the particular feature of said entity. Through this capacity the affection is transferred to the somatic innervation—to the real of the body—a wretched product of an intolerable representation.

It's common in clinical analysis to observe in women, even after years of analysis, a marked resurgence of symptoms when they're faced with moments of their children's growth. When they leave their parents' home, when they finish school or college, or when they get married.

There is a regrowth of hysterical suffering, which phallically invests in her body, in her symptoms, a child that she had given birth to long ago.

The place of the son bridged by the phallic enjoyment that, without any propitiatory doubt regarding the creature in its instituting moments, will later symptomatically become a conversive enclave of the mother's body.

The clinical case that I will present next seems to me eloquent enough to show how, even though at the beginning of analysis the subjective constitution is a subsidiary of the boundary of the enjoyment of the primordial Other, the trajectory toward approaching the barred female position, which in this particular case was reclaimed, through the intervention of the analyst, a subtraction in that favored place of settlement of the phallic enjoyment, a boy.

When Helena arrived for consultation she was a fifty-eight-year-old woman with three sons. Two of them were married, and one still lived with her and her husband. She was a teacher in all the different levels of education, and she occupied management positions in renowned educational establishments.

She was consulting after an economic venture failed that consisted of realizing a long-awaited aspiration: opening a partner school with other colleagues, in which she had invested most of her life savings.

In the beginning of the analysis, she started describing an array of ailments, some of them being leftover from illnesses that she suffered in her childhood. One was the fatigue that accompanied her during various times of anguish, and that she linked to the frequent asthma attacks in her early childhood. Another one was severe pain in her legs. There weren't any doctors that could find an etiology for this, although they had prescribed numerous and painful injectable painkillers.

Among her constant grievances of not finding a place to be, a grievance that covered different aspects of her life, but that lately had reverted to not finding a place to work as a professional. A memory leaks of her never having a room for herself. She grew up sleeping in her mother's bed all through her childhood. Finally, when they moved to a bigger house where they promised her that she would have her own room, her older brother, who was recently married, took the room. In order to not return to the maternal bedroom, she slept on the couch in the living room.

Among other gripes about her mother, we'll mention the fact that she repeated the sixth grade due to constant absences. Her memories associate it with a feeling of profound humiliation, and the nickname they gave her, Penny, the name of the coin with the least value.

She always felt loved and attended to by her father, although when comparing him to her mother, the absence of his presence stood out in the story.

There was a dream that was repeated: "I got into the water and enjoyed it, I wasn't afraid. I felt the water on my body. Somebody was holding me, and I learned how to swim and could make it the other shore."

She drew from that dream that it was about her desire to swim that she had as a child, even though she was afraid of swimming. She believed that when inside the water, she wouldn't be able to breathe. She would get in, and then get out frightened.

She related swimming with enjoying her body. Not drowning like with her asthma attacks throughout her childhood. Swimming was being able to breathe peacefully in the water. In the dream, the water was set up for her as a nonthreatening space where she could move around, which was very different from the primordial Other that suffocated her, not granting her a place besides her own bed.

Phonematically, she associated swimming ("nadar" in Spanish) with the body becoming nothing ("nada" in Spanish), relieving it from those troubling pains and fatigue, which she repeatedly attributed a lot of her impediments to.

After some appointments and analysis, Helena had achieved placing herself differently regarding aspects that afflicted her in the beginning. She wasn't submitting herself to the needle pricks from the injections anymore, which she realized were only placebos. She started to counsel educational establishments. She moved easier around unsolved questions "without drowning inside a glass of water," as she repeated frequently.

Nevertheless, and this is particularly what I wanted to refer to, as the moment where her younger son was deciding to move out got closer, there was an acute reactivation of the symptoms, leaving her again imprisoned in an aching body. Fatigue and pain in her legs reappeared with an intensity that had ceased long ago.

On one occasion she entered the office complaining, and, referencing her fatigue, she said, "It's not that I have shortness of breath, it's that I can't disembarrass (TN: 'desembarazarme' in Spanish, as in become unpregnant) myself from it."

I told her that it's time to disembarrass herself from her youngest son, who had already turned twenty-five.

Right there from the divan she started to exhale heavily, disembarrassing herself from the air that overwhelmed her, but she also seemed to hyperventilate as is needed when having difficulty in labor, even with the intervention of the analyst.

After that peculiar session, another stage in the analysis started. In a couple of sessions, she started by remembering that she forgot to bring and show me a notebook that she prepared for the schools that she advises, which she had enjoyed doing a lot. She said, "It's divided into three bodies, what appears in one is missing in the other" and she described with great detail how she organizes her work with that guide.

On one occasion, before leaving, she told me that when faced with a setback, she waited for the fatigue to come. Though her face wielded a wide smile, she seemed surprised when she said that it didn't come; it failed her.

It was a moment in the analysis where, through the creation of a notebook, she spoke about bodies where the absence is inscribed, and the ones that start to miss the session are fatigue and pain. It was a gradual announcement of the beginning of the end of the analysis.

This clinical material served me for coming up with some reflections that reformulate the questions about femininity, taking into account the contributions made by Lacan. When it comes to articulating them with the theory of enjoyment, what relationship links and unties hysteria and femininity? What is, in the end, the purpose of the analysis of what is feminine? Would there be another conversion to process? Without wanting to exhaust the subject, we'll make some observations.

Lacan, moving forward from his return to Freud, dislodged hysteria from the enclosure of psychopathology and granted it a status of discourse.

From that discursive structure—the hysterical woman's discourse—a new relationship with language is revealed, a social bond that gives birth to the position of the analyst.

It's in that mode of organization regarding desire, as the dissatisfied desire, linked to the insatiable and inexhaustible question directed to a Master, that resides in the suffering dimension of the hysterical question, of the feminine enigma. It's the discourse of the hysterical woman that, placing the cause in the place of the truth, is fruitful for the access to a certain knowledge, a metonymic knowledge of the unconscious.

The course of an analysis probably starts out from the attempt to decipher the enigma that the ailments of the hysteria encloses, in their innermost being, and proceeds toward the indicator, that when truth is emptied from all its senses, what remains is only the sense of the truth of emptiness.

That's why we place that which concerns the enigma, which would keep it eternally in the question, awaiting a signifier that would grant them a knowledge that would give her consistency as a woman, on the side of hysteria. We propose, instead, that moving forward toward femininity in the final stretches of analysis requires extracting the letters of what is mysterious about that enjoyment, which is particular to each one of them—that is, it doesn't make a discourse. It's the enjoyment that nestles in the unfathomable void, around which the body interweaves itself. Mystical and mystery are both terms derived from the same Greek root *myo*, hidden, shut. Would it be in this aspect, this mysterious one, that such extra feminine enjoyment that Lacan also called mystical is related to what the mystics described and wrote about as their singular meeting with God?

As is taught to us using the Borromean knot throughout the Seminar XXII, *R.S.I* (1974–1975), the symptom is an excessive ostentation of the phallic enjoyment, that, as the heading says, a son, through the symbolic place he occupies in the feminine equation, can saturate. The subtraction of the phallic enjoyment, vectorized by the analyst, in its resumption clears up the place intended for the absence. It's an intervention in the real of the mother's body that fosters an unfolded distribution of enjoyment. A knowledge of what to do with the mystery of their body.

It's the pathway of analysis that, through the analyst's desire, allows them to track down the letters that remained lumped together in the family novel, and, by rearranging them, will offer them a reading to "know how to create" another writing with them.

POSTPARTUM PSYCHOSIS: A REJECTED MOURNING?

The anemic conditions that take place immediately after birth frequently has a close link with those for whom mourning arises. Sadness, abulia, an attitude of libidinal introversion that doesn't express the socially expected joy because of the arrival of a baby frequently stain the first encounters between a mother and her son.

Without a doubt, giving birth is a mourning that touches the real of the maternal body. In accordance with the structural disposition that the mother has regarding the instituting lack, she can accept such a separation, or she will exhibit the ailments of her vicissitudes.

The phenomena that take place on occasion present characteristics of a psychotic break. There are hallucinations and delusional ideas with reference to the baby, such as he is possessed by spirits or condemned to a deadly fate.

In other words, the postpartum period is, as with any other significant loss, a moment in which the structure is tested to its maximum regarding its constitutive frame and its symbolic resources to make the instituting lack available.

When hallucinations of a visual or auditory nature and the ideas of the delusional type are manifested, they can lead to the mother rejecting the newborn, or even harming him in some way. Auditory hallucinations, frequently of imperative content, can order to kill the child.

Our hypothesis is that during the difficult mourning involving birth, there can be manifestations of psychotic phenomena, but that are subsidiaries of *Verleugnung*—denial—and not of *Verwerfung*—foreclosure.

They are two ways of responding to how intolerable the separation of their bodies is, which speak about the forms of making the absence in the structure available. Without a doubt its consequences will fall to the *infans*.

Next, I will recount the first interviews of a woman that came in for consultation extremely anguished because of how unmanageable the severe episodes of violence of her teenage son were, and which ends up causing her to tell the episode of postpartum psychosis which occurred immediately after the child was born.

Lucía, a forty-seven-year-old woman, arrived very anxious. In her first few interviews, she ascribed her severe anguish to the disturbing relationship that she had with her older son, seventeen-year-old Bruno. He was violent, aggressive, and constantly exposing himself to situations that put his life at risk. She described everyday scenes where, faced with small disappointments, he destroyed the first thing that crossed his sight. He physically and verbally abused both his parents and his younger brother.

In one of her first interviews, Lucía reported,

> I got married in 1974. I was 26 years old. My husband is much older than me. He is of Scandinavian descent. One year later I got pregnant. A few months after that the hemorrhage started. I had to be on bedrest. I was taking antispasmodic medication right up to the end of the pregnancy. At that time I lived with my mother-in-law. In their house everything worked perfectly. They called me "the spoiled one" because of my health issues. My mother-in-law told me that her brother fought in World War II. That when he was taken prisoner, they cut his head off because he was "very hard-headed." Bruno has their blood. He's also very hard-headed. He was born with a double nuchal cord. When I saw him I thought, "that kid is terrible." I thought that he was the reincarnation of his great-uncle. Then I started to yell and see images of Rome, of the places I visited on a trip I did when I was a teenager. I saw the Trevi Fountain. They brought me the baby to hold it, and I started to scream that they take him away, that I didn't want to see him. They injected me with 10 mg of Valium.

Bruno took Haloperidol, an antipsychotic, from two to six years old. When asked due to what symptoms, she answered that when his tower of cubes would collapse, he'd start to hit his head against the floor.

She kept on describing Bruno's teenage years. During that stage, he started to insult his mother—he called her a whore, a slut, a "sidosa" (pejorative term for someone who is HIV-positive)—and threaten his father with a knife during violent arguments. On some occasions he also broke appliances and furniture with a mace he built at his industrial school.

One of the incidents that took place prior to Lucía's session consisted in Bruno wanting to get out of the house, but he couldn't find the keys. After an outburst where chairs went flying through the air, he left slamming the door. Lucía said that the keys were on the floor next to his bed. She explained, "What happens is that sometimes Bruno can't see. He can't see anything at all."

When I responded, "It'd be good to help him see" she answered, "I feel like he died."

It had been a few months since Bruno no longer lived at his parent's house. He lived with his maternal grandparents. He only resorted to violence and risky behavior in the presence of his mother. Strikingly, and in contrast to what took place in his family, he was loved in all the places he frequented. He worked at an optical shop and wanted to study to become an optician.

We know that in Seminar XI, *Four Fundamental Concepts of Psychoanalysis* (1964), Lacan formulated that the emergence of the subject is in the place of the Other and related to two foundational functions: alienation and separation. Through such functions the interval that will give birth to the subject, that interval where the subject is always between signifiers, is generated. That the subject finds themselves between signifiers makes it so that in their constitution, they manifest themselves as barred, elided, reinventing themselves permanently.

In a situation of real separation, as it is with birth, the way in which the lack in the structure and the faults or vicissitudes of inscription in the instituting moments functioned are manifested in various clinical phenomena that accompany the postpartum period, and in which it can be read the mode that the structure has to process the losses, when these represent profound narcissistic wounds.

In neurosis, faced with what is experienced as a loss, the subject responds with the phantasm. We could say that they respond complaining about their phantasmatic reality. In the melancholic position, it would seem that the phantasm fails to respond and sentences the subject to a permanent grievance in which they become their own worst enemy. As Freud says in *Mourning and Melancholia*, their complaints are really "plaints." "Their complaints [*klagen*] are really 'plaints' [*anklagen*], in the old sense of the word. They are not ashamed and do not hide themselves, since everything derogatory that they say about themselves is at bottom said about someone else" (Freud 1957a, 248).

That constant boycott which the melancholic is confined to guarantees the consistency of the Other, an absolute and devastating Other.

NOTES

1. See the clinical excerpt allusive to this topic in "Femininity and Its Mysteries" in this chapter.

2. Marie Magdeleine Chatel (1994), in her article "In the Absence of Havoc, a Folly of Publication," mentions a guilty enjoyment with respect to the maternal–filial relationship, which would impede that the propitiatory separation occur.

3. "Relationship" understood as "rapport,," which in French means proportion. "*Il n'y a pas rapport sexuel*" as "There is not a sexual proportion," what takes precedence is the difference, the radical discord.

4. If Freud proposed that there are some psychical consequences because of the anatomical sexual distinction, paraphrasing the homonymous article from 1925, it's to propose that in the first place that there are consequences . . . of the distinction. This brought feminist movements to devaluate these affirmations, lowering the enriching idea of "distinction" to the degrading "inequality." We believe that the Lacanian aphorism "*Il n'y a pas rapport sexuel*" is a renewed way to refer to the differences, the diversity, given that it indicates the disproportion that always governs in relationships between the sexes, between the expected satisfaction and the attained satisfaction. Even more so when the love between the *partenaires* naively supposes that the "two" will become "one." It's needless to say that within one there is no distinction.

5. Juan David Nasio, in a personal communication, distinguished different specific objects for which mourning usually took place for people in feminine or masculine positions. For women, he pointed out that it of first concern was being abandoned by a loved one, distinguishing that for them, the possibility of a loving relationship entailed love being an exercise in and of itself. Love is an object. In contrast, men consider preeminent the wound the image itself incurs. Pain due to humiliation is typically more masculine.

6. *Diccionario de uso del español*, "cópula," by María Moliner (2007).

7. See Lacan, J. (1978) "The Transference and the Drive" in *The Seminar of Jacques Lacan: The Four Fundamental Concepts of Psychoanalysis: Book XI*. New York: W.W. Norton & Company.

8. I wrote it in Roman numerals and was surprised by the coincidence between the Roman numerals used to identify the seminar and the pair of chromosomes used to designate a female.

9. Translated by Gabriel Sarmiento.

10. This text was presented at the Founder's Meeting for a Lacanian Convergence in Barcelona, 1988.

BIBLIOGRAPHY

Freud, S. 1955b. "On Transformations of Instinct as Exemplified in Anal Erotism" in *SE, Vol. XVII*, 125–34.

Freud, S. 1957a. "Mourning and Melancholia" in *SE, Vol. XIV*, 237–58.

Freud, S. 1961a. "Some Psychical Consequences of the Anatomical Distinction between the Sexes," *SE, Vol. IXI*. 243–60.

Freud, S. 1961b. "Female Sexuality" in *SE, Vol. XXI*, 223–46.

Kierkegaard, S. 2014. *The Concept of Anxiety*. New York: Liverlight.

Lacan, J. 1999. *The Seminar of Jacques Lacan. Book 20: Encore 1972–1973, On Feminine Sexuality, the Limits of Love and Knowledge*, New York: W.W. Norton & Co.

Lacan, J. 2006. "The Signification of the Phallus" in *Écrits: The First Complete Edition in English*. New York: W.W. Norton & Co, pp. 575–84.

Lacan, J. 2014. *Anxiety: the Seminar of Jacques Lacan, Book X*. Cambridge: Polity.

Moliner, M. 2007. *Diccionario de uso del español*, Madrid: Gredos.

Chapter 4

Mourning for the Father

WHEN DOES THE FATHER DIE?

> Your son will prove by nature admirably endowed with many valuable gifts; nor will the lessons which have now been impressed on his mind be from thence ever wholly effaced. Though the passions of his sinful father should boil and ferment in his veins, yet by proper education their influence might be repressed, and he might even raise himself up to be a valiant champion of our holy faith. Let him therefore be a monk!
>
> —E.T.A. Hoffmann, 1824, 7–8

From the myth of *Totem and Taboo* (1913), when the father is overloaded by enjoyment (*jouissance*), it is presented as the *pére-version*, creating the conditions for his murder by his descendants. Indeed, if they kill him, he dies, but this is not why we could argue that he is positioned in the structure as a dead father, rather tending to outlast his children. He had to be killed, which, quite to the contrary, did not negate the effects that his presence imposed but that these, after the criminal act, were reinforced. The father's function could only be faulty, and this is what gives rise to the *pére-version.* There are different ways in which the paternal function is faulty, depending on how the father faces up to the real in which there is no sexual relationship. The *pére-version* can be the ferocity, the arbitrariness, the weakness, the boasting, the severity of his gaze, his obscene noises, the perpetuation of being in the position of a son in front of his own father. This *pére-version* exceeds the symbolic function of the father. It makes the real of the father, which only with difficulty could be passed to him, find its reasons. It concerns his enjoyment.

The murder engenders a flashback of blame and, in this way, the father and the effects that this causes are perpetuated in the subject's structure. The murder is a way of taking the father back in time, so that the real father operates, summoning in him the imaginary, the symbolic and the real versions of the father. As it's exposed in the myth, it's essential that the act of homicide—the murder—is carried out so that the father's law regenerates the structure in another way, regulating the enjoyment. The father's murder opens up the possibility of grief for the father, founding the mythical, exceptional father, the one that the subject cannot avoid "provided that he makes use of him."

Following Philippe Julien's proposal in *Le manteau de Noé* (Noah's Mantle) (1995), there are three dimensions according to which a subject reaches filiation. The symbolic dimension, from which he receives the Name-of-the-Father—his surname. It's the mother who establishes this third position between herself and her son, indicating that he is the father of her child. Thirdness makes the symbolic function of the father. The imaginary dimension, which is how every child begins to build a paternal image, covers what every subject assesses as the potencies and impotencies of the father. It's what's unraveled during analysis. That the father, during childhood, was seen as being of tall stature and worthy of admiration. Then, other idols replaced him: heroes from television, teachers, politicians, leaders, or erudite teachers. The third dimension is that of the real father, who is the one that introduces the category of the impossible, who comes to convey that there is a constituent impossibility that all knowledge corresponds to, which is said in an absolute way and who also experiences this impossibility. He is the father agent of castration. The third one is the father who, instead of imposing himself on his son as a holder of truth, enables him to know what to do with the lack. He is a father that knows he is mortal and therefore can pass on his inheritance so that he leaves a legacy. He empowers his son to be able to make the arduous journey of mourning for the father, a father saturated from childhood with imaginary vesture.

In his Seminar XVII, *The Other Side of Psychoanalysis* (1969–1970), class on March 18, 1970, Lacan posited: "The father's death. In effect, everyone knows that this appears to be the key to, the vital point for everything that stated, and not only in the name of myth, concerning what psychoanalysis is about" (Lacan 2007, 119).

Let's remember that, in the first seminars the relevant emphasis for the watershed moment with respect to the structure given over to the significance of the Name-of-the-Father and the paternal metaphor. In the most advanced ones, it's modal logic and the quantifiers of sexuation which support its function as an exception. In knot theory, *sinthome* is proposed as what comes from replacing the absence of the Name-of-the-Father, while the main road in the subjective structure. The subject of the father's death offers letters to, toward the end of the analysis, open the floodgates of what mourning for the father implies. Both the imaginary and idealized father, as well as the symbolic father that imparts the law and intercedes between the mother and her progeny. This bereavement of the father strengthens the real father, while resizing the operation of castration.

We don't propose exhausting this topic in these few lines, but to posit some reflections on the father's function, specifically that of the real father—the agent of castration—and his scope in terms of the final parts of an analysis.

In the year 1963, between Seminar X, *Anxiety* (1962–1963) and XI, *The Four Fundamental Concepts of Psychoanalysis* (1964), Lacan started a seminar that was called the *Name of the Father*, which he did not finish but resumed ten years later in a seminar called *Les non dupes errant*. He took advantage throughout the seminar of the phonemic homonymy between what could be translated as "the names of the father" and "the non-dupes err."

The plurality of the Names-of-the-Father is not insignificant. Lacan himself said so. The seminar was asking, why this plurality concerning the names? Although he didn't give an immediate response, he follows with the story told of Isaac's sacrifice. Citing chapter twenty-two of Genesis, which tells that Abraham did not sacrifice his son and, in place of this, God demanded that he sacrifice a ram, which is an animal ancestor. He emphasizes what is an ancestor, and therefore, not a descendent. I would like to underline that we could interpret that a child does not die sacrificially, someone from the descendancy, when the father god abstains from extreme, excessive enjoyment. It's in this context of the relationship between God and Abraham that, in place of a sacrifice, the initiation rite of circumcision is established. Symbolizing a small sacrifice, a pound of flesh which is surrendered as a compromise of alliance with the people that it belongs to, and which for the Hebrew religion inscribes a subject onto their father's lineage, from their identifying marks.

This start to the millennium received from Western modernity a model of father who sways between two extremes. One is the traditional figure that affirms the standards of paternal authority, frequently slipping away from authoritarianism and the imposition of extremely arbitrary mandates in the name of the law. On the other extreme, where it seems that they are launching a teenage rebellion against this model that they themselves have received, we find parents that, idolizing youth, mimic their children, and seem completely disorientated in carrying out their function.

Between both extremes, the paternal role calls to be recreated according to current times. Both the strict traditional model and the one that we see in the present day, in which the father as a subject does not prioritize his place as a man that passed the threshold of adolescent fluctuations to the complex function of the father.

Today, crossing through deep transformations in relations between the sexes, and with scientific-technological advances that have revolutionized methods of procreation, the father, the role of the father, will require a multiplicity of names through which to carry out his function?

The plurality of the names of the father seems to foresee, in the aftermath of the century, the backing of the complexification of paternal destiny instead of the crystallized patriarchal univocity of other times. Said plurality of names of the father is a subsidiary of the concept of the real father, the father agent of castration, who carries out his function in a propitiatory way because it brings his lack into play. It's the father who prioritizes assuming the risks of creatively learning what rearing his children is like while adopting an overused, instituted, and out-of-date model.

There's the totalitarian omnipotence of the father at one extreme, and his impotence at the other, which delivers his children to be sacrificed. Both positions conceal the role of the real father as impossible. An impossibility that resists the truth being shown only in the registration of a symbolic articulation. It's the distance between holding knowledge of what it is to be a father and the true meaning of this function.

The symbolic role of the father has its paradigm in the Name-of-the-Father, an essential element of the paternal metaphor, which primes the pump through the significations of a subject. He is the son of a name; it's through giving a patronymic that the paternal filiation is forged.

A fragment of the Talmud relates, "A person has three names: one that he is called by his father and mother; one that people know him by, and one that he acquires for himself." The last one shows the scope of the real of the father that contributed to subjectivity.

Lacan calls the real father a structural operator who gathers in the center of the experience of analysis the modal category of what is impossible. In this way it occupies an exceptional place, a delicate function that consists of imparting the law without embodying it.

It's a unique position that does not lead to making a model of the father, but instead enabling the subject to take a gamble and produce their answers there where the letters of the father's name weren't able to write a knowledge about that of which there is no possible knowing: sex and death.

The real father knows how to carry out his function because he admits that his knowledge doesn't reveal the truth. He is the agent of the act; he is the father of what is real because castration is a symbolic operation of maximum effect on what is real.

When does the father die? Will we be in a position to respond? When the son is not admonished to the sacrifice of giving himself absolutely to make him exist, at any cost, as the father, it perpetuates the son in his condition as a son.

Returning to the title of the present text, the question of the father is key to understanding the paths of a subject, up to that point where the sin of the father boils over. In the direction of the cure, arriving at the limit in which the father's enjoyment raises an unknown specter, lets himself be bound by the letter and promotes a meeting with a real father. The analyzer, in this way, is freed from this quota of paternal enjoyment which comes over him as (*pére-version*), like an immutable debt.

Although the name of the father governs the structure, at times the subject stays perpetuated in the place of the son, without being able to grieve for the father figure, as he is already permanently waiting for a father to carry out their function, which also has devastating effects. The following clinical material tries to tie up some questions about this topic.

Roberto came in for consultation as he was approaching turning forty. He had just finished—*finished off*—a wholesale business which he had been running for years with the help of his wife. Being that his patronymic contains the same letters as the name of a game of chance, in the first interview he said,

> For a year it seems like I've been "a player" with the business. I started taking on debts, listening only to what I wanted, I raffled it off. I don't understand what happened. Then my wife told me to leave the house and I consented.

Being the youngest of three brothers, his parents separated when he was four years old. His father moved to a city in the interior of the country, where he had built another family. He told how, though he continued seeing his father, on one occasion, when he traveled with his older brother to that place and called his father to visit him, his father stated that they could not go to his home because the children from his first marriage *did not exist* for the new family, "not now . . . *perhaps later on.*" Offended and hurt, both brothers cut off their relationship with their father.

Shortly after this episode, his older brother contracted a serious malignant disease and died. When the father was called to let him know, he said that he wouldn't be able to attend the funeral. Roberto said that for him, his father died at that moment. He said, "It was always like that, he didn't think about us, we didn't exist for him. We were that stupid child that he had to hide away."

During this time, as he seemed to say in his story, the financial debacle began, the failures, the losses, the gambling, everything. He said, "This turned on the blender for the business accounts." Almost identifying himself with the death of his older brother, he added, "It was financial suicide."

Recently settling into a new professional task with which he was very comfortable, he was entrusted with traveling to the city where his father lives. He started to become anxious, with the anxiety taking the form of bodily discomforts and breakdowns. He referred to knowing that his father had two daughters from his new marriage, and that he needed to know who they are and meet them. First, he toyed with this idea, then he said that he's going to leave it for *later on*. On this occasion, I interrupted the session, asking, "Still later on?"

This intervention precipitated what he had been procrastinating, a postponed act. He decided, although not without hesitation, to write his father a letter, announcing his upcoming arrival in that city and reiterating, after many years, that yearning that had been put on hold to meet his new family.

In response to the letter, he got a phone call from his father, in which he invited him to dinner at his house. The reencounter with a father of flesh and blood—"real"—began, that, being much closer, eases the fall of imaginary consistencies that left Roberto confined to permanently being the son, in the agonizing wait for a father to finally recognize his existence.

THE SUICIDE OF A PARENT

Some bereavements are more difficult to get through than others. The suicide of a relative, a parent, spouse, a son, or sometimes someone that unites some familial relationship, adds to the sorrow of the loss a huge dose of guilt that's extremely hard to remove. A third period of mourning, that finally makes it possible to consummate the loss a second time, that is, when what was lost in the real is lost for a second time in the symbolic, is extremely hampered.

Let's talk about a clinical case. It's about a young woman who came in for consultation at twenty-four years of age. Her professional studies had been stymied because she couldn't pass a basic course for her major: pharmacy and biochemistry. Once she had failed the exams and then prepared to take them again on subsequent occasions, upon reaching the door of the university building, she was overrun by panic that made her leave without taking the test.

At one point, she began to recount how her father died when she was fifteen, and that for many years she thought that it was because of a heart attack. Many years later, though, she found out that he hanged himself in the chemical laboratory that he owned. Her mother told her abruptly during a fight they were having. She was very shocked by this, but she denied it, and only recently having begun the analysis began to tell it and with much difficulty. She was trying to protect a mother that had no problem attributing a certain hint of blame to a young lady in those fights that began to ensue.

Telling this family secret in the analytical device, where the transfer is made, allowed her to attain an essential relief, in the sense of being able to do something with it. In addition to crying and grieving, rescuing paragraphs from her family history led her to recovering forgotten letters which can be used to subjectivize the loss and register it as absent.

The function of mourning keeps the value of subjectivizing the loss that it be recorded (in the sense of attaining a possession) and registered as missing. It's losing the object again, consummating the loss for a second time, and producing in the symbolic, through subjective means, what happened in the real.

Shortly before passing her biochemistry exam, a signifier that weighed on her because of the relationship she had with the chemical factory where her father had committed suicide, she had a dream, "I'm in my boyfriend's car, and an intruder gets in through the back door and locks the doors so that we can't leave and then threatens us with a gun." In the dream associations, it surfaced that being unable to advance in her studies because of biochemistry was closely related to her father and his suicide in the chemical factory because of an economic collapse. It was linked to not being able to move forward, held in a guilty enjoyment.

Upon finishing her studies, years of analysis later and after becoming a bride-to-be, while being very excited because of all the wedding preparations, she made a statement, already nearing the completion of her analysis, that disclosed a position opposite to what had brought her in to be analyzed,

> Actually, I don't know if I'm going to be able to forgive him for dying, for having committed suicide so young. Did he not think about me? Did he not want to see my growth as a woman, as a professional?

We can say with certainty that it's not that he didn't want to. It's that he couldn't. It's that the fragility of the structure in the face of adversity threw him into a *passage à l'acte*, although this reproach directed at the deceased helped her to reverse the phantasmatic position.

Recapping the consultation, she was impeded on several levels in her life. The hole in the real caused by her father's death had sent her into a position of deprivation. From that deprived state, the guilty feeling stained all the areas of her existence. It obstructed her in all of her endeavors. The questions that she began to form revolved permanently around that topic. Why had he committed suicide? What could she have done to avoid it? How did she not notice his state of severe depression? Why had she not spent more time with him?

A set of self-reproaches that usually haunts the relative in the face of a death caused by suicide.

Several years after the completion of that analysis, I found in that reversal—the question was no longer about what she didn't do to prevent it, but why he couldn't accompany her as she grew—how to respond with another ghost, from a different phantasmatic position to a family tragedy.

Moustapha Safouan, in an unpublished text where he comments on Jean Allouch's *Erotics of Mourning in the Time of Dry Death*, expounds extensively on the topic of mourning. There he makes an interesting observation that, for Freud, his father's death was such a marked event because of the amount of work of symbolization that it set in motion, as is testified in *The Interpretation of Dreams*. Regarding the replacement of the lost object, Safouan emphasizes that it's precisely because the loved object is irreplaceable that it unravels into a series of infinite substitutions. Another of Safouan's interesting reflections is that he argues that every mourning is about encountering a truth, though that truth isn't always necessarily the same. But it's a truth that always concerns the structure more than the person or the psyche.

We understand, then, that the work of mourning is the occasion to access a certain knowledge about the limits of the structure, about the moment when the object was constituted. It fosters a change "of the object itself," as Lacan says, of the phantasmatic relationship of the subject with the object.

I'll allow myself to digress briefly to address the issue of guilt, a feeling that persistently stains mourning, and even more so when it's the result of a suicide. We understand guilt as the maximum imaginarized expression of enjoyment. In the relationship between a mother and her son, it's a paradigmatic operating method. It's particularly common to see it with first time mothers. In reality, boys sometimes play, "Can you lose me?" They hide, do some mischief, hit themselves to test maternal distress. In the breastfeeding stage as well as their early years of life, this is a condition of the phallic-libidinal investment of the baby. Nonetheless, maternal distress due to fear of loss can sometimes be excessive and impacts children, leading to symptoms. In *Note on the Child*, Lacan says, "The child's symptom is located in the position of a response to what is symptomatic in the family structure." He then concludes, "The articulation is much more limited when the symptom that comes to dominate arises from the subjectivity of the mother. In this case the child is directly concerned as the correlate of a fantasy" (Lacan2018, 13).

The child's "can you lose me?" and the anguish that it causes the mother produce a symptomatic response in the children, which corresponds to the mother's display of guilt that translates into reproaches that we could express as: "Where did I let them down?"

From Mourning to Invention

Let me introduce three quotes which we will try to interweave. First, in the Preface to the second edition of *The Interpretation of Dreams*, Freud says:

> For this book has a further subjective significance for me personally –a significance which I only grasped after I had completed it. It was, I found, a portion

> of my own self-analysis, my reaction to my father´s death- that is to say, to the most important event, the most poignant loss, of a man´s life. Having discovered that this was so, I felt unable to obliterate the traces of the experience. (Freud 1971, XXVI)

Jorge Luis Borges in his "An Autobiographical Essay" recalls:

> It was on Christmas Eve of 1938—the same year my father died—that I had a severe accident. I was running up a stairway and suddenly felt something brush my scalp. I had grazed a freshly painted open casement window. In spite of first-aid treatment, the wound became poisoned, and for a period of a week or so I lay sleepless every night and had hallucinations and high fever. One evening, I lost the power of speech and had to be rushed to the hospital for an immediate operation. Septicemia had set in, and for a month I hovered, all unknowingly, between life and death. (Much later, I was to write about this in my story "The South.") (Borges 1971, 170)

And finally, Walter Benjamin in his "Death of the Father" states:

> But from this day onward he worked with less certainty. Deficiencies became apparent; fundamental problems, which up until then he had regularly glossed over, began to preoccupy him. His book orderings would suddenly lose all reason. He was surrounded by piles of periodicals, in which he made absurdly painstaking searches for the most unimportant pieces of information. When not absorbed in reading, he never lost the feeling of a man whose clothes are too big for him. (Benjamin, 2011, 130)

As we previously described, the term "mourning" was coined by Freud for psychoanalysis in 1914, with the writing of the famous essay *Mourning and Melancholia*. Freud defined mourning as the reaction to the loss of a loved person or some equivalent abstraction, among which he mentions one's country, liberty or an ideal, and he proposes an elaboration, a work of elaboration, *Trauerarbeit*, to remedy said loss. It's a process that would conclude with the shift of the libido toward other objects.

In *Mourning and Melancholia*, logical times of mourning can be found, three periods for the elaboration of the loss that I'll briefly describe here.

The first period is where the shock produced in the structure by the loss sends the subject into a position of denial concerning the object. It can be universally observed that man doesn't willingly abandon a libidinal position, and various phenomena attempt to annul what reality affirms. Naming the loss is a way of locating its place in relation to the subject, that the subject can orient themselves around the new condition that befalls the object, that of being inexorably absent.

A second period is accordingly that of elaboration, the symbolization of what was lost. It comprises the detachment of the libido piece by piece, requiring a great investment and expenditure of time and energy. It's accompanied by a painful displeasure.

And the last period, which can be found in the text, where the libido, after regaining self, if it's not a pathological mourning bogged down in melancholia, is available to be attached onto other objects of love, replacing the lost object with another.

Up until now, these have been brief notes on *Mourning and Melancholia*.

Lacan returned to and reexamined that essay on successive occasions to make progress on this topic, and to propose, as I understand it, an essential function of mourning: extracting from it the threads to channel the desire. The function of mourning is to propitiate the subject's access to a desired position. Here we already find the first development regarding this issue.

I want to highlight that for elaboration, a proposed work of the psychic apparatus, to process the traumatic aspect of mourning so that the mourning fulfills an enabling function for desire, a shift occurs that, to me, seems to be of great interest to set one's sight on the cure.

From this there are some consequences that can be deduced in clinical studies that I'll describe here. The pathological ways that mourning—consistent with the moments where it stalls—is manifested not only includes depression, lack of interest in the environment, loss of the ability to love and functional disorders that we know of that affect appetite and sleep, but also a varied range of alterations in the ability to do things that range from generalized inhibitions—procrastination—to impulsive and erratic kinds of actions known as acting out and *passage à l'acte*.

This last point is the one that I'd like to emphasize, and to propose that if the function of mourning operates, it promotes the opportunity for subjective reregistration. It's a reregistration of the fundamental lack, the emptying of enjoyment that the subject of the act engenders, subject to their story that promotes a know-how that doesn't stop itself in its inhibition, nor does it precipitate the impulsive mode of acting out.

What I think is important to note is what Lacan says was his only invention—the object designated by the first letter of the alphabet—that is, the object *a*. To my understanding, it's what grants the object its status that allows it to address the logic of mourning because it's an object that swivels between additional enjoyment and cause of desire.

Mourning because of a father's death is particularly special as far as mourning goes because, as the authors cited in the bibliography indicate, it's a death that draws up a "before and after." It's the particular moment in a subject's life where the traits received from the parents, the legacy sustained and the heritage to be passed on will be resignified

"Invention," that which a subject can create, doesn't carve out in their existence something apart from the inheritance that they have received from their predecessors, as Goethe's well-known verses say.[1] But appropriating it for oneself implies rediscovering it, recreating it, and imprinting one's own style upon it.

The cited authors refer to that irreparable loss differently, but all of them recognize it as a transcendent milestone in the existence of a man. Both Freud and Borges describe it from the autobiographical experience, and having known how to forge a recognized and meritorious name in their respective disciplines, they seem to give merit to their parent, distinguishing that moment that was so significant in their lives.

The inspiration for the title of this section "From Mourning to Invention" came from a beautiful autobiographical novel from Paul Auster called *The Invention of Solitude*, which he began upon hearing of his father's death.

It's a novel that consists of two parts. The first is written in the first person; it's called "Portrait of an Invisible Man." The second one, written in the third person, is called "The Book of Memory." Both of them tell of memories from the life of the author and his father. They are memory fragments that try to reconstruct the relationship between father and son. I picked this book because, throughout the story, the different times of mourning previously detailed are unraveled. From the beginning, where he describes his contact with the dead man's belongings with a deep sense of strangeness, it complies with what we call the first period of mourning:

> When that life ends, the things change, even though they remain the same. They are there and yet not there: tangible ghosts, condemned to survive in a world they no longer belong to. . . . I kept expecting my father to walk in, to stare at me in disbelief, and ask me what the hell I thought I was doing. (Auster 2007, 8–9)

The second part, "The Book of Memory," written in third person as if trying to create a distance, seems dedicated to that fine work of elaboration which requires the awakening one by one of the memories that tied him to he who was absent, and carry out the piece-by-piece detachment of the libido.

He brings up multiple memories of repeated greedy behavior on his father's part in a series of daily deeds that brought him to deprive himself from several joys, and Auster as the son to be frequently embarrassed by that attitude during business.

Recalling those memories, as Auster mentions, safeguards him from the terror of silence, since he states that when he dips one foot in silence, that will mean that his father has disappeared forever. Through remembrance, a father is revealed that is characterized by appearing invisible, to the point where he says of him, "He never talked about himself, never seemed to know there was anything he could talk about. It was as though his inner life eluded even him" (Auster 2007, 18).

Throughout the novel he recounts various events from his father's story that he will discover as a way of elaborating the bereavement: he learns that his paternal grandfather had been killed by his wife. Also, almost with an autobiographical style, he tells of his travels, talks about his partner, and shares about his relationship with his son Daniel. He seems to be trying to reconstruct his place in the world, in the family tree, with a need to pass it on to his child.

The shift that can be seen in Paul Auster is interesting, a product of the death of his father: to make a permanent reference to the father by addressing his son, naming himself as a father.

> When the father dies, he writes, the son becomes his own father and his own son. He looks at his son and sees himself in the face of the boy. . . . For it was only at that moment, he later came to realize, that he had fully grasped the full scope of his own fatherhood: the boy's life meant more to him than his own. (Auster 2007, 79)

The plot of the novel opens the dimension of his conversion into his own father, as a result of loneliness and a look directed toward his son.

The death of his father demanded *The Invention of Solitude*. But there is a fourth moment in addition to the three previously indicated, and it's the period of the act of writing. The writing of the book, its publication, contains a real dimension. He says,

> and before it [a word] finds its way to the page it must first have been part of the body, a physical presence that one has lived with in the same way one lives with one's heart, one's stomach, and one's brain. (Auster 2007, 138)

In conclusion, "From Mourning to Invention" points to traveling along a course. The bid is that mourning be the exquisite opportunity to recover some letters of the lost story to write the "family novel." Beyond the replacement of the lost object with another, mourning compromises a logic of the supplementary, a decided act, a know-how, an event which inscribes the letters with which a subject names themselves.

FREUD BEYOND CHARCOT: *ÇAN'EMPECHEPAS DE EXISTER*

In 1893, J.M. Charcot died, who Sigmund Freud had initiated his studies with about the human psyche.

The clinical practice in the Salpêtriere Hospital and the lessons the teacher gave were the seeds and incentive of Freud's first theoretical developments on hysteria. The obituary that Freud wrote on the one-month anniversary of his precursor's passing away thoroughly shows the impression left on him from working together with Charcot. Even though the path the creator of psychoanalysis created distanced itself considerably from that of his teacher, he redeemed episodes of everyday life with him and his particular liking of clinical observation from that experience. There he repeats a phrase that he didn't translate—and precisely because of this it acquires a singular value—that Charcot used to respond to his students when the symptoms that the patients exhibited didn't fit the symptom picture described in the books. Freud depicts a memory that, in my view, has bequest value for the generations of future analysts; in fact, it appears that he led the way to separating from psychiatric nosology and founding psychoanalysis, the discipline that finds indelible traces in the symptoms of the singular, alphabetical making of a subject.

On one occasion, where he was gathered with his students debating about a clinical case, one of them commented, "That can't be because it contradicts the Young-Helmholtz theory." To which Charcot responded, "La théoriec'est bon, maisçan'empêche pas d'exister"[2] (Freud 1962, 13), emphasizing that the clinical case and its nuances always take precedence over the theory. Being careful with the singularity of each case seems to be a priority in the teaching of the clinic study which the teacher profused.

It'd be interesting to take this Freudian testimony into consideration when the term "borderline" tries to group clinical entities together in a nosology that are simply forms of presentation of neurosis today, in accordance with the endorsements that the era and its particularities imprint upon it. If psychoanalysis hadn't extended its know-how beyond clinical borderline personality disorder, it would've restricted its scope of action to standard neurosis, the neurosis that was already outlined, to that which was already condemned to the field of the "unanalyzable," the modalities of ailments that the coordinates of each era imprint on the subjectivity. That wasn't the Freudian spirit, nor that of his successors. Difficulties in establishing transferential ties, the demand for immediate solutions and extreme impatience from those that are supposedly "patients," an absence of phantasmatic life, actuations, risky impulses, addictions, and somatizations are the forms of presentation of suffering that require of the analysts interventions that operate in the register of the imaginary, symbolic, and real. The future of psychoanalysis places under consideration the desire of the analyst to foster a "subject effect" where the social imperatives appear to try to abolish it. They are times of extreme subjective haste that demand to reflect on the clinical practice, make it dialectical, and question the theory again in order to not dogmatize it. The implicit challenge of analytical doctrine inexorably consists in operating in a field where there is always a gap between the theory and clinical practice, between the referential knowledge and the literal knowledge of the text, and between the conceptualized ailments and the inventive multiplicity of the symptom.

In the obituary for the death of he who had been his teacher, Charcot, and in his own autobiography, offers said episode as a memory of an unforgettable force in the face of the surprises that clinical practice in its singularity offers, and before the objection of his disciples that the said cases didn't appear, nor were they outlined in any nosography of the time. Charcot responded plainly, *Çan'empêche pas d'exister: That Doesn't Prevent it from Existing.*

It's a phrase that Freud doesn't translate, but remembers as untranslatable. As such, it appeared in the order of that which Freud could make use of. It's a phrase that clearly contrasts that which for Charcot was "characteristic" of the clinic that was to "see and organize," "do nosography," "find the clinical picture." If said untranslatable phrase did cling to Freud, he mentions it repeatedly in his work, it was probably because of the propitiatory effect it had on him. It was a transmission effect from a paternal place. It's like that which a father transmits unknowingly, which stays in the air, waiting for his successors to take it—to take it on—to continue forward.

What he took from he with whom he began his activity, and with whom he came across the real of clinical practice and studies, was this phrase. He made use of it to go further than the father and to found in a short time, following the path of not yielding to desire, the praxis that we are bound to.

NOTES

1. What from your fathers' heritage is lent, / Earn it anew, to really possess it!
2. "The theory is good, but that doesn't prevent them from existing."

BIBLIOGRAPHY

Auster, P. 2007. *The Invention of Solitude*. New York: Penguin Books.

Benjamin, W. 2011."Death of the Father" in *Early Writings (1910–1917)*, Cambridge, Massachusetts: The Belknap Press of Harvard University Press, 128–31.

Borges, J.L. 1971. "An Authobiographical Essay," in *The Aleph and Other Stories*, New York: E. P. Dutton & Co., 135–85.

Freud, S. 1962. "Charcot" in *SE, Vol. III*, 11–23.

Freud, S. 1971. "The Interpretation of Dreams." *SE, Vol. IV*.

Hoffmann, E. 2007.*The Devil's Elixirs*. London: Grosvenor House Publishing.
Julien, P. 1995.*Le manteau de Noé: essai sur la paternité* [Noah'sMantle]Paris: Desclée de Brouwer.
Lacan, J. 2007. *The Seminar of Jacques Lacan: The Other Side of Psychoanalysis, Vol. Book XVII*, New York: Norton.
Lacan, J. 2018. "Note on the Child" *The Lacanian Review*, no. 4, 13–14.

Chapter 5

Mourning and the Body

MOURNING AND THE BODY IN PSYCHOANALYTIC CLINICAL CASE STUDIES

> "Mourning is regularly the reaction to the loss of a loved person, or to the loss of some abstraction which has taken the place of one, such as one's country, liberty, an ideal, and so on." Freud says in *Mourning and Melancholia* (Freud 1957a, 243).

In the face of a loss—a loss that concerns existence—it's common to observe the different subjective positions at the clinic when someone is faced with something missing and the failure to register it as absent.

We say a loss that concerns existence—a hole in the real—since it isn't a common loss for which a subject would be in mourning. It's a hole in existence, but, precisely and paradoxically, existence not with regard to their surroundings, but that which alludes to their most intimate story, that is, the one that touches their very core.

And thus, we quickly enter into the topic of the body. Freud continuously asked himself about the painful nature of mourning. In *Draft G*, he described the rupture of associations that are required for mourning as an internal hemorrhage. Similarly, he finished the classic 1915 text alluding to the distinction that would be befitting to consider between physical and psychic pain.

Freud picks up the subject again ten years later when, in the last section of *Inhibitions, Symptoms and Anxiety*, he proposes an instructive differentiation between anxiety, pain, and mourning (Freud, 1959a). There he establishes that the pain subsides into physical pain. And that this involves a high narcissistic burden that "empties" the self. Let's remember Wilhelm Busch's verses, which Freud quoted in *On Narcissism*, "Concentrated is his soul. . . .

In his molar's narrow hole" (Freud 1957a, 82). He refers to the physical pain that compromises the real body, or rather, the real things of the body.

From this point a question arises regarding mourning, as it's a painful reaction that arises under the influence of the examination of reality, which definitively imposes a separation with the object since it doesn't exist anymore: *In which body does the mourning hurt?*

I propose to think that in mourning the imaginary body hurts, a topic extensively discussed in the last part of this chapter. There we state that the pain caused by mourning is the result of an intrusion, an impact, a plus in the mirror image, i(*a*), when the object no longer operates in the place where it's missing (−φ), but as an absolute presence. "For whom shall I adorn the image returned to me by the mirror if the object responsible for love is lost?" could be the overt question of the one who lies in a melancholic mourning. We say that the object functions as an absolute presence because, although lost, paradoxically, it's still a permanent object in the mind.

The pain that takes root in that imaginary body where mourning hurts is where the different conversive or organic expressions of mourning, stalled in their periods of processing, come from.

I propose to consider that, when faced with a loss, the subject elaborates a *response*, and thus we enter into the constellation of the conversive symptoms. If one doesn't have symbolic resources with which to respond, one *reacts* with what is organic and real.

Answering is manifesting or expressing oneself to satisfy a question or proposition; it is a resource against the immersion in helplessness that a blunt loss produces. *Answering* is also responding to a name, to a particular call that defines a singularity. The symptom is a response addressed to an Other person, a response that needs to be deciphered. It's an unconscious formation that encloses a message. It has signifying materiality, by which the classical interpretation, through the symbolic, makes a dent. It manifests itself in the sense of the recognition of desire, although in an illegible way at first. It calls for a significant recomposition in which the letters that nominate a subject are sorted and stabilize their phantasmatic knotting. Let's remember that in the previous records of psychoanalysis, those from *Studies on Hysteria* (Freud 1955), often the onset of conversive symptomatology was linked to a serious illness of the father, his decline as an ideal, or his death.

In this line of study, Elisabeth von R.'s case is exemplary, where the sadness, the pain, the burden, and the anguish that the disease and then the death of her father caused for that young woman converted itself into a precise location on her body.

"Why was it that the patient's mental pain came to be represented by pains in the legs rather than elsewhere?" Freud asked in the epicrisis (Freud 1955, 174).

Elisabeth's leg was a facilitated channel for the symptom because of the repeated times her father had held up his wounded leg there for her to carry out the treatment, thus creating a localized somatic complacency. On this she brings together and imprints conversely the play on words: *Stehen-Alleinstehen* (standing-standing alone). Standing, when her father was brought to her after the first heart attack; then standing in front of her sister's casket, standing and unable to advance a step and feeling very alone, wanting to reassemble the family harmony after two successive and unrecoverable losses, the death of a father and a sister.

The leg pain corresponded in Elisabeth to a transmutation of a psychic pain into a somatic pain, overdetermined by the fixation that, as she finds her decipherment, it produces a bounded enjoyment in favor of access to a knowledge of the unconscious.

A *reaction* is the way to repel an attack or aggression. Unlike an answer, it's the apt reflex of a living being versus a stimulus. In this case, there's an immediate manifestation and a step that isn't used, the resource of questioning oneself.

This is what Lacan refers to, when talking about psychosomatic phenomenon. He makes use of the Pavlovian experiment.

The main condition for a conditioned reflex is the coincidence over time in one or more instances of an indifferent stimulus (the bells), with an absolute stimulus (the food). This results in an alteration of the biological order, and that in the face of indifferent stimulus, an inadequate reflex or reaction is obtained—salivation.

Lacan proposes that, at the level of the composing moments, there has operated an equivalence between signifiers, holophrasis, which does not result in the subject being represented by a signifier to another in the chain. The signifiers, subtracted from their essential function—of registering the pure difference—and, instead, functioning as equivalents don't promote the aphanisis of the subject.

Such signifiers function as the bells of the experiment, promoting a reaction that is an alteration of a biological function. This way of reacting when the signifying induction doesn't promote a subjective response is what, under the aegis of repetition, will give occasion to the psychosomatic phenomenon.

In the "Lecture on the Symptom," M. Vauthier comments that when one gets the impression that the word enjoyment acquires a psychosomatic meaning, then it ceases to be enjoyment. Next, Lacan states that it's by the revelation of the specific enjoyment that is in their fixation that it should tend to approach being psychosomatic (Lacan, 1989). We can hope based off of this that the invention of the unconscious can be used for something.

It is necessary to have in mind that this specific enjoyment is immeasurable; it's related to a particular name given to the psychosomatic phenomenon that is the epistemo-somatic failure. It alludes to the effect that science's progress will have on the relationship between medicine and the body. If there is a failure in this relationship, a gap, it's because the increasingly sophisticated technology allows to explore, measure, and inspect that body to its most remote places, but there is a dimension of that body which is impossible to quantify, which is the dimension of the enjoyment. A specific enjoyment that has become embodied, and is of the order of the disembodied, the untouchable, and the immeasurable.

Already in its presentation there is a dimension of self and nomination that combine themselves in those who suffer from a psychosomatic condition. I have asthma. I have hypertension. I have psoriasis. I have cancer. They're ways of forming one's identity (TN: In Spanish, all of these conditions would appear as predicate adjectives; for example, I *am* asthmatic, I *am* cancerous). It's the dimension where the Name-of-the-Father as the father that names is absolutely abolished for the subject.

THE BODY AS THE PROTAGONIST: HYSTERIA, HYPOCHONDRIA, PSYCHOSOMATIC PHENOMENA

Lydia is a twenty-eight-year-old woman who is married and has two children (Nicholas, three-and-a-half years old, and Martin, one-and-a-half years old).

She comes in for a consultation with her husband. When she comes into the office, she says that five years ago she began to have a discomfort in her throat, as if she had swallowed a whole hard candy, which makes her feel like she's suffocating. "I haven't had a bite of food in five days," she says. She's also very depressed, she's having a hard time getting things done at the house, and she's too afraid to go out or be alone. "I think something could happen to me. I don't know, get sick, die."

She's gone to a lot of doctors and healers so that they could tell her what's in her throat. She believes that it's cancer, though the professionals repeatedly tried to convince her that she didn't have cancer, and that the problem was all in her head, calling her a hypochondriac. Lydia went on to have several studies, X-rays and even endoscopies to corroborate her own diagnosis. The results were always negative.

Crying and distressed she said, "Everyone tells me that I don't have anything, but I'm sick. I'm getting worse and worse. What do I have? Please don't tell me I have nothing," she asked with fixed insistence.

I replied that she had several things to say, some related to that suffocation, and others that have to do with her, beyond those discomforts in her body. An intervention that aims to produce a change of registration, like the "you don't have anything" of the doctors, becomes something unbearable. It's better to have something, even if it's cancer. Having or not having, phallic or castrated, an imaginary game that alludes to the dynamics of castration.

She then remembered that there were two occasions when the discomfort subsided, and almost disappeared completely: it was during her two pregnancies. But after the birth of the second child, everything got worse (she would later say that it was actually when Martin started walking). She added, "Since then I have pains, and half of my body falls asleep. It usually happens to me at night when I lay down." In addition to this there was tightness in her chest, palpitations, and restlessness. "So, the same thing always happens." Then she described the following scene, "My husband gets up, goes to get my mom to stay with the boys and takes me to the clinic. There they gave me Valium, and this whole part became numb." As she's pointing to the places she says, "My throat, the roof of my mouth, my jaw, my whole tongue. It was even difficult to speak."

Almost systematically, these early interviews began with one of these statements:

"I went to the cardiologist. The EKG was normal. He told me I don't have anything."
"I went to the clinic. . . . I go to clear up my doubts. Next week I have an appointment with the neurologist."

And they always ended after a series of complaints and regrets with the question: "But are they sure I don't have cancer? [. . .] Shouldn't I have more exams done?"

On one occasion, she came in very distressed. She had been coming by herself for a while. She mentioned that this time she found the trip very troublesome, that she doubted whether to continue or get off the bus and return home. She was overrun by a very intense fear of dying. "Now this throat thing won't leave me at night or during the day," she says.

After my question about when this annoyance had begun, and whether she could relate it to any significant event around then, she repeated once again that it began five years ago. It was shortly after she got married, and she didn't remember anything important. However, now she added, "Well, not right at that time, but almost a year before, a few months before I got married, an uncle of mine died of throat cancer."

"I went to visit him with my mom. She hadn't seen him in years." (She says that her mother walked away from her family when she got married. She said that they were all kind of screwy, and that actually, this one was the only one of her brothers she saw again shortly before he died.)

"I can't forget that image in intensive care. He was lying down, and you could see his throat that was opened. Seeing it open like that was what shook me the most. Doctors said they'd never seen a case like that. He died in October, and I got married in March." She added, "And yes, maybe that influenced what I feel. If you have an appendix, I look at you, and then I have an appendix."

She continued,

> At that same time my paternal grandmother died. She had senile dementia. I was just looking after her when she died. Poor old lady! She did everything. She would dirty the bathroom wall, run away, say that Mom hadn't given her anything to eat. It made me want to suffocate her.

I intervened, "The one who started suffocating soon after was you."

She's surprised. She told me of a few more incidents with this grandmother, and then said that recently she learned that her maternal grandmother had died in Spain, where she had gone to live with an uncle of hers. She added, "But nobody is taking this idea from me that I have something in my throat, even if the last endoscopy I took was fine. Do I have to have another one?"

In another interview she brought a big pin on her blouse with the phrase "Enough with routines."

She said that she had a pretty bad time over the weekend, that it was always the same thing. Her husband proposed to go out with her, but she preferred to stay to clean the house:

> I'm not going you anywhere. I like for everything to be dressed to the nines. I was thinking about the boys. It makes me sick to leave them. I don't leave them with anyone except for my mom. Anyway, the other day when I got back, the youngest's butt was red and the oldest didn't want to eat.

She talked about how unbearable she finds it being locked up with them all day: "They get everything dirty all the time, they get on and off the table. If they're not fighting, they're watching TV. They seem drugged."

I said, "Some of this is reflected in the pin you're wearing." And I asked her if she hadn't thought about sending the oldest to kindergarten.

"Yes, I enrolled him. I paid for the registration," she said. "The first day he stayed with no problems. My stomach hurt a lot. After an hour and a half, I went to pick him up before it was over. The next day it was all screaming. He cried all the time. The teacher said to me that he said, " 'I have to go take care of my mom.' After that I didn't send him anymore."

"It seems that it was more difficult for you than for him to be separated for kindergarten," I pointed out.

She said,

> Yes, for me leaving him for a while is like I'm missing a piece of me, an arm, a leg. It's the same with Martin. I was very close to my mom, too. I don't let anyone near if my mom doesn't know. If I'm missing my mother, it's maddening. When I got married, I cried all the way from here to Mar del Plata. I realized on the train that it was the first time I was going to be apart from her.

Over the course of the interviews, she told me how, as a girl, she was always taken to the doctor.

> They called me the little girl in the glass box. I was sick all the time. I went to the dentist a lost. I always had cavities. They would sit me down, give me anesthesia, and I would run away. I was shaking and no one could hold me down. I have all false teeth except for two or three.

She also mentioned something her mother told her to tell me:

> My mom was in a lot of pain when we were kids (she and a brother three years older); she cried all day. My paternal grandmother was one of those Galician women who bossed everyone around, and my mom had no voice, no vote. We cried at the foot of the bed with her. When my mom got sick and nervous (headaches, fainting, depression), we left to live alone. My children see me crying all day, too. I cry you, and I cry you, and I can't stop. I feel very lonely. My husband works all day, until eleven at night. He tells me to not count on him.

When I asked her about her father, she said he wasn't in the house much because he was traveling. Then they fired him, and now he doesn't have a retirement pension. She says:

> He was very jealous. I had to be home by eleven. When I was 15, I started dating, and when I was 17, I had an abortion. I wanted to die, my mom had never told me anything. When I found out, I was three months pregnant. My mom, dad and my current husband accompanied me. I don't know if it lasted ten minutes or ten hours, but I felt it all, a terrible pain. . . . Up until then I had only had one throat operation. I remember they put a huge rubber bib on me and that a big guy with pincers came near.
>
> Thus far, a fragment of the clinical case. A series of interviews.

Lydia is a patient who comes mainly to complain about a discomfort, a suffering in the body, her throat. It's somewhat similar to what Freud describes for us in his first clinical cases of hysterical patients. Emmy, who had muscle contractures and aches in one leg. Katharina, who had difficulty breathing, suffocation, and tightness in her throat and chest. Elisabeth who had intense pain in her legs (Freud 1955). Dora who had multifaceted symptomatology linked to orality: coughing, aphonia, dyspnea (Freud 1953b).

They're clinical records where the body, moving to the front and center, is the explicit reason for consultation, sometimes adding other ailments. On these occasions, the body breaks the silence to which its image confines it to present itself as pain, oppression, paresis, tremors, or laments.

There are a number of issues that were raised in the interviews with Lydia, certain signifying indicators that made me question whether it was a hysterical conversion, or some other entity where the body also expresses itself, whether it'd be hypochondria or a psychosomatic phenomenon.

Just because there's an ailment in the body doesn't mean that a symptom has presented itself there, in the way in which psychoanalysis considers it. Only if from this condition a question comes to be where the subject themself becomes an enigma, an interrogation that addresses not only the enunciated (the descriptiveness of the suffering), but mainly the place of enunciation (overdeterminants that place the subject at the mercy of the desire of the Other), can a demand for analysis be heeded and initiated.

This question doesn't always come out in interviews. The patient isn't always able to prioritize the effects that the discursive deployment produces and distance themselves from their organic suffering.

The attitude Lydia showed with regards to her symptom was the exact opposite of what we call *la belle indifférence* of hysterical woman, in which an extraordinary conformity, according to Freud, relates to pleasurable thoughts and sensations linked to such conversions. She was dominated by an intense fear of death and an almost certainty that she had cancer in her throat.

When she talked about this, there was a cessation of associations, or when she recalled memories (I'm referring to the traumatic experience of her uncle's throat cancer or her grandmother who she wanted to strangle), Lydia seemed to remain oblivious to her own association and would again maintain that "there are moments when no one can convince me that I don't have cancer. Don't you think I should have more tests done?"

We'll try to point out some differences between the three entities mentioned: hysteria, hypochondria, and psychosomatic phenomena.

In hysterical conversion, the body considered is not the one learned about in anatomy. Instead, it's the body of representations. It's a symbolized body. It's not the cuts that the neural network made that determine it, but the cuts that took place in the relationship between the subject and the Other of the signifier. The symptom, by being a formation of the unconscious, has a language structure, which assumes being subject to the laws of condensation and displacement (metaphor and metonymy). This makes interpretation effective so that, in its signifying materiality, it employs effects of decipherment and modifications to it.

Hypochondria (which is a label that Lydia carries with her after repeated consultations with specialists) is an entity that Freud considered in various works. In his first works of 1895, he already cited it along with the current neuroses (neurasthenia and anxiety neurosis). He refers to these neuroses being associated with an unreasonable fear of dying, or something catastrophic happening to their loved ones, proving that they are irreducible through psychoanalysis because the mechanism of substitution (read condensation and displacement) is not applicable, since the anxiety that accompanies them doesn't come from a repressed representation of their sex life, as is the case with hysteria.

In the neurotic person, the incorporation of the language and of the Name-of-the-Father by means of the paternal metaphor has an effective effect on the organism by producing the separation between body and enjoyment, confining the latter to certain zones called erogenous. With hypochondria this doesn't occur, and the organism as real appears inhabited by the enjoyment. Another way we can say this is that the body has not been mortified by the signifier, as in the "the word kills the thing" mode. The anxiety of today's neuroses lies in the presence of the unlost body in the field of the signifier.

Twenty years later, in *On Narcissism* (1957a) and then in Chapter VII of *The Unconscious* (1957a), hypochondria is placed next to paraphrenia (schizophrenia and paranoia). In the latter, he cites the example of a schizophrenic patient for which the phrase "her eyes were not right, they were twisted" (Freud 1957a, 198) presents a hypochondriac character comprising what he called "organ-speech." He added that a hysterical patient would have "in fact" convulsively twisted her eyes. In *On Narcissism*, he points out that with hypochondria, there is a retraction of the libido in the ego parallel to an alteration in the erotogenicity[1] of the organs.

While for hysteria it's an unconscious fantasy that is located in the body, with hypochondria the possibility of translation of the unconscious system to the conscious fails because the primary repression has not been registered correctly. The patient frequently builds a delusive metaphor for the organ they claim is affected in a restorative attempt.

We'll say a few words about psychosomatic phenomena. Already its denomination of phenomenon announces that it's easier to describe it than to resolve from theory in which structure to place it in: neurosis, psychosis, or perversion. This extraterritoriality enables the possibility that as a phenomenon, it can appear in any of the three structures, provided that there is a bodily injury related to a psychic disturbance.

Lacan in the Seminar XI, *The Four Fundamental Concepts of Psychoanalysis* (1964) includes it in a series along with mental weakness and psychosis. In these entities the S1 is holophrased to S2, leaving no interval where the subject can go to. "A signifier represents a subject to another signifier" (Lacan 1978,157). In this statement what is proposed is that the subject is something to be represented. There are two logical operations of constitution of the subject in relation to the place of the Other: alienation and separation, which enable subjective causation, that the subject appears as missing, desiring, aphasic. In the psychosomatic phenomenon, the welding of S1 with S2 submits the subject to a kind of petrification, of monolithic constitution, which is unpronounceable in relation to an Other that isn't the propitiatory Other of the signifying battery, but an Other as a body, not mediated in the symbolic.

The preceding development is a theoretical journey that allowed me to locate the coordinates for a diagnostic distinction.

Lydia has expressions where her body manifested itself insistently from the Real, almost as if in pieces: a throat with cancer, if she sees an appendix, she grows one, the numerous cavities, her children being like an arm or leg to her.

She also used expressions, some quoted in the records such as: "I ate you a ton," "I cry you all day," "I'm not going you anywhere," where verbs that are intransitive become transitive, and those that are transitive take the interlocutor as an object, becoming incorporated into the action.

Despite these particularities, the manifestations were defined in the field of conversive symptomatology.

The interviews continued, and the analytical device operated for the transfer to emerge, where Lydia will recognize a cause for her symptom, which she ignores, but whose knowledge she assumes is of an Other. In principle it manifests itself in that insistent question: "Are you sure I don't have cancer?" To which I practically refrain from replying. Slowly, from the complaint, from the suffocation, from the suffering placed onto the body, she begins to be distressed by other issues. Something she brings in that has a phrase—"Enough routine"—begins to be able to be talked about. Arguments arise with her mother, and on weekends she allows herself to go out for a while, even if the house is not "dressed to the nines."

A PRELIMINARY QUESTION TO ANY POSSIBLE TREATMENT OF PSYCHOSOMATIC PHENOMENA

From Phenomenon to Symptom

Once again, in "Analysis Terminable and Interminable," Freud highlights a limit to the psychic field. It's about the one that fills the biological field, which as an underlying bedrock makes an impassable barrier to be crossed by the action of the word.

A place of the real that gives us the direction to approach what it means when he places psychoanalysis among the three impossible professions.

If we want to be precise, the living organism whose bedrock doesn't coincide with the body unified by the mirror image, nor with the body of members articulated in its posture, in its walk, in its kinetics, by having been impacted by the articulated word; the body of the symbolic.

From the beginning, the body had a prominent place in psychoanalysis. To move forward, let's go backwards a little and ask ourselves: What concept did Freud inherit from the science of his time? That which was taken from Cartesian dualism, *res extensa*, radically separated from *res cogitans*.

Clinical studies on hysteria warned Freud that this is not strictly the case. The suffering of his patients, the conversive symptoms, expresses, through the body, repressed unconscious representations.

The term "conversion" indicates that the detached libido of the representation is transferred; it becomes a somatic innervation that follows a purely phantasmatic path, not obeying the pathways prefigured by the anatomy.

Thus, this modality of late-century hysteria was widely recorded in Freudian clinical records, a time when the body barely stuck out among the bulging apparel. Today referring to a culture where image predominates, where the display of the body and aesthetic surgeries of all kinds are common, hysteria, with less of an appearance of *belle indifférence*, in keeping with the time, seems to hum, paraphrasing the poet, "Look at me, look at me and don't touch me, but look at me."

The relationship with the body at the end of the century is different from that of the present. Thus, hysteria continues to produce symptoms, in line with the discourse of the time, which is a characteristic of the symptom as a formation of the unconscious.

It's important to note that with hysteria we talk about the *formation of the unconscious*, to differentiate it from a phenomenon (a term that comes from Greek and means "what appears, that which is placed before all beliefs and denotes what is given"). We are talking about phenomena also as in psychosomatic phenomena, where, instead of a commitment formation, there is a lack of commitment to discourse, which makes its clinical entities, such as asthma, cancer, psoriasis, hypertension, ulcers, autoimmune diseases, and others that continue to fill the series, be preserved through the eras almost unchanged. Nonetheless, they occupy a specific place in the clinical structures that make nosography psychoanalytic: neurosis, psychosis, and perversion.

The symptom, while a formation of the unconscious, is a counterpart to language, which involves being subject to the laws of condensation and displacement, functioning as a metaphor and metonymy. This makes interpretation effective so that, in its signifying materiality, it employs effects of decipherment and modifications to it.

This is not the case for psychosomatic phenomena, where we often see the interpretive game limited, and at times the need arises to ask ourselves, "where is the subject?" when they appear only signified by what is dramatic in the condition that harms them, and which also ends up identifying them, showing up as: "I have an ulcer, I have asthma, etc."

Holophrasis: Welding the First Dyad of Signifiers

To enter into entities such as psychosomatic phenomena, mental weakness and psychosis, is to reach the limits of our field. Lacan proposes that the first pair of signifiers become solidified, holophrasing between S1 and S2, leaving no interval for the location of the subject in the experience of the discourse.

Holophrasis implies a particular relationship of the subject with the signifier that isn't without consequences in its relationship with its own name, with the object *a*, the real body, and the enjoyment.

Let's refer to these two operations that Lacan proposed to talk about the causation of the subject in the place of the Other: alienation and separation. These operations are the logical support of the subject's emergency and the expulsion of the object. Let's see where they fail so that, where an interval should occur, there is a weld, or solidification, that doesn't allow the subject, blocked, divided, and desiring, to precipitate into the interspace.

We understand that these operations open up a path to think about the advent of a subject in accordance with the intervention and failures in the intervention of the signifier of the Name-of-the-Father, as long as it's nominating, at a first instituting moment, as well as the paternal metaphor at different and successive logical moments of that becoming.

It's necessary that the signifier of the Name-of-the-Father has operated in that first instituting period as a letter in the real, so that it's then available as a privileged term in the equation of the paternal metaphor to establish, each time, once again the lack in the Other.

Alienation is that first operation that places the *infans* before a forced election. They either choose being (and it remains in the immanence of being the phallus of the primordial Other), or they choose the meaning, at the cost of disappearing under the weight of the S2, remaining aphanisic, in *fading* but represented in the chain.

To illustrate this underlying logic that makes the causation of a subject, in which, regardless of the choice they end up making, something is always hopelessly lost, Lacan refers to the Hegelian dialectic "your money or your life." And he just states it as: "There's none of that . . . without the other thing. Synthetic statements that also concern the practice that we are encumbered with."

For this choice to occur by meaning the signifier of the Name-of-the-Father must have operated to establish phallic significance, effecting the subtraction of at least one signifier, the phallic signifier.

We call this movement the signifying induction, which implies an opposition between S1 and S2. Having this S2 (*Vorstellungsrepräsentanz*) be the effect of producing the aphanisis of the subject.

The problem with psychosomatic phenomena is that, citing a paragraph from Seminar XI, *The Four Fundamental Concepts of Psychoanalysis* (1964):

> The psycho-somatic is something that is not a signifier, but which, nevertheless, is conceivable in so far as the signifying induction at the level of the subject has occurred in a way that does not bring into play the *aphanisis* of the subject. (Lacan1978, 227)

What signifying induction is this that, "at the level of the subject," doesn't bring into play their aphanisis? It's an induction that doesn't promote the particular function of the signifier in the subject, that is, registering the pure difference. At that point in the chain, an equivalence between signifiers persists.

It's in the second operation, in which we recognize the *Ichspältung*, or splitting of the subject, in which the subject brings into play, if they had any, their aphanisis. In the face of the desire of the Other and their hesitations, the subject attacks the chain, offers their disappearance, and places themselves within the question, asking: "Chevuoi? What do you want?" It's the paternal metaphor that in the operation of separation establishes the absence in the Other in the same movement that the lock of the subject carries out.

In psychosomatic phenomena, having not put in play the signifying induction, the aphanisis of the subject, as in Pavlov's experiment of conditioned reflection, the S is not questioned by the desire of the Other. There is an equivalence between signifiers that has the effect of disrupting biological functions.

The Body Carrying Its Own Name

We propose that it isn't strange with psychosomatic phenomena for the mode of operation of the signifier of the Name-of-the-Father as the Nominating Father that a specific enjoyment is imposed. It's common for these patients to experience their own body, in their condition, as a piece of a body that doesn't belong to them, as the body of another.

The equivalence between signifiers remits us to consider it tantamount to the concept of frequency in reference to natural numbers.

For these numbers it's different to occupy a place in the series, between a predecessor and a successor, which tells us about an operator (the 0 as an absolute absence) that drives the progression, than for that number to repeat successively, a repetition of the identical, such as a bell being run every 30 seconds. Here the number is only a figure that is repeated in equal intervals.

Thus, the signifier of the Name-of-the-Father operating promotes the subject function. The signifying chain is equivalent to the 0, absolute absence, for the set of natural numbers. It drives the progression, but without the chain, we wouldn't be able to say anything about it.

The signifier of the Name-of-the-Father, the letter in the real that gives a surname, a trace of identity for the subject, is the one that inscribes the subject in the generational lineage as someone to be numbered by an ancestry and for a descendancy.

It seems that in psychosomatic phenomena, the signifier of the Name-of-the-Father doesn't promote that place for the subject as the 0, absolute absence, the place of the impossible. The equivalence between signifiers predominates, and "the body lets itself go to write something of the order of the number" (Lacan 1989, 23). We could say it's a figure, being one of the connotations of this last term "monogram," a drawing of initial letters of the name.

Some organ seems to be responsible for restoring the symbolic exclusion of the proper name through a bodily injury, in which the subject, at the price of a disease, concretizes within itself something of their "being," establishing an incarnated affiliation, without signifying mediation.

Psychosomatic Phenomena and Anguish

Is it possible for the subject who creates a psychosomatic phenomenon to question themselves through the desire of the Other, to get involved in their own condition, when, as we said, there had been no aphanisis from the subject?

I think this is closely linked to how one manages their anxiety during the course of an analysis. It's closely linked to what is stated in Seminar X, *Anxiety* (1962–1963): "Anxiety is thus an intermediary term between jouissance and desire in so far as desire is constituted and founded upon the anxiety phase, once anxiety has been got through" (Lacan 2014, 175) and to that aphorism that postulate that "[anguish] is not without object" (Lacan 2014, 242) for it's a sign of a certain moment of the relationship of a subject with the object *a* in all its generality.

Psychosomatic phenomena, by not putting the aphanisis of the subject into play, puts into play a relationship with the object *a*, where, it not having

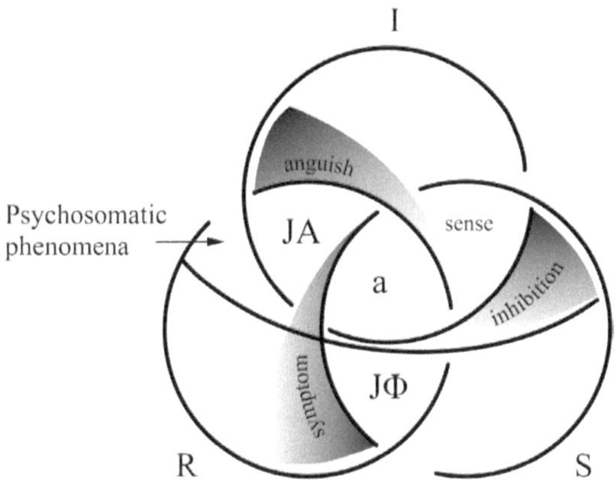

Figure 5.1 Psychosomatic Phenomena in the Borromean Knot. *Source:* Created by the author.

fallen, the object presents itself embodied in a specific enjoyment. "It's from this angle, it's through the revelation of the specific enjoyment that he has in his fixation that one must first of all approach the psychosomatic. This is where one holds out hope that the unconscious, the invention of the unconscious, can be of some use" (Lacan 1989, 23), we read in the Geneva conference on The Symptom.

We think that this may be the way to phantasmastize the somatic injury and relocate it into a relationship with a question, modifying its subjective position.

If you ask about the desire of the Other, "Chevuoi?" it causes anxiety, an anguish indicating and speaking to a dialectic put in play between the subject and the Other. This is a resource that one who suffers from a psychosomatic condition doesn't appear able to recur to.

The subject answers, it would be more accurate to say reacts, as Freud described it when referring to current neuroses, with automatic anxiety (which he ends up calling toxic) which also causes conditions in the body (digestive disorders, respiratory disorders, headaches, weakness).

A coincidence between *current* neuroses and psychosomatic phenomena is this kind of response, *current*, without the intervention of anxiety as a signal, almost at the same level of the reflex reaction in Pavlov's experiment.

As is aforementioned, and because the psychosomatic phenomenon affects the real body but is "fundamentally, profoundly rooted in the imaginary" (Lacan 1989, 23) we propose, in a Borromean knot, which is found at the beginning of the Seminar XX, *R.S.I* (1974–1975), to place it in opposition to anxiety, that is, in a shaded area in which, departing from the imaginary, it covers the ring of the real.

EPISTEMO-SOMATIC GAP: BETWEEN DEMAND AND ENJOYMENT

On February 19, 1966, Lacan, at a round table at the Salpetrière, called "The Place of Psychoanalysis in Medicine," he warns those who were listening to him about an ethic put at stake when it comes to what is called psychosomatic phenomenon.

An ethic which, as far as analytical work is concerned, must delineate two benchmarks. On the one hand, there is the patient's demand for their suffering to decrease, often after several unsuccessful treatments. On the other hand, there is the enjoyment of the body, a body that in its enjoyment presents itself as alien, a body of an Other. An abysmal distance extends itself between the two of them, demand and enjoyment, which is unavoidable to consider when it comes to that specificity of the phenomenon embodied in the body.

Lacan proposes the term "epistemo-somatic gap" (*faille épistémo-somatique*, [Lacan 1966, 766]) to indicate the failure of the theory of scientific knowledge in its advances and progress to achieve a knowledge about the human body. The organism, so long as it can have enjoyment, always exceeds the *res extensa* of the cartesian dichotomy.

This epistemo-somatic gap alludes to the effect that science's progress will have on the relationship between medicine and the body. Although increasingly sophisticated technology allows you to explore, measure, inspect, and photograph that body to unsuspected extremes, the dimension of the enjoyment is inextricably immeasurable for it.

If there is an essential distinction between the symptom as a formation of the unconscious and the psychosomatic as a phenomenon, pertaining to what can be deduced from the analytical device, it's to foster a twist where what's phenomenal, that which impacted and injured the body, can find a place in the discursive plot and produce a symptom in transit. That it may be historized, placing that before and after, finding those key moments of the becoming of a subject where words weren't able to achieve communicating the traumatic real and the impact on the real body.

"I was speechless." "I ran out of words." These are some of the phrases a patient uttered after having suffered a *heart attack* in the face of an economic exasperation caused by his "bosom friend," as he put it.

"My guts were all twisted," was the catchphrase of a woman in the face of everyday disagreements. This time she said it while lying outstretched on a bed in a sanatorium, referring to a recent painful episode, after having undergone surgery for the eighth time for repeated *blockages in her intestines*, even though there wasn't any worthy medical cause to justify it.[2]

The concept of an epistemo-somatic gap makes the belief that the advances of science would always result in greater well-being for the body waver.

However many scientific advances or refinements are achieved, what always escapes the scientific universe is the enjoyment dimension of the body. This dimension is often on the edge of pain, suffering, and other deadly sensations; the limits at which the body can experience itself in an exceptional way. From an ethical position that recognizes this discorporate dimension, the wager is on the dialectization of that which was embodied as a phenomenon.

Phenomenon is a term that comes from The Greek and means what appears, that which is placed before all beliefs and denotes the given. If we propose that in its historization the psychosomatic phenomenon is made dialectical, it's so that, through associative chaining, it can manage to dialect and build an argument, to make itself phantasmatic.

This way the space to read out a letter that lay dead, frozen, holophrased. And which presents itself breaching the mucous membrane as in an ulcer, obstructing airways as in asthma, branding the skin with scales as in psoriasis, or invading tissues with a rush of cell proliferation as in cancer.

To specify criteria for a diagnosis through psychoanalysis, we rely on the definition taken by Lacan in Seminary XI, *The Four Fundamental Concepts of Psychoanalysis* (1964). There he says:

> The psycho-somatic is something that is not a signifier, but which, nevertheless, is conceivable in so far as the signifying induction at the level of the subject has occurred in a way that does not bring into play the *aphanisis* of the subject. (Lacan1978, 227)

As we previously developed, what signifying induction is this that at the level of the subject their aphanisis isn't put into play? It's an induction that doesn't foster in the subject the primordial function of the signifier, that is, to represent it in the chain for another signifier by registering it as a subject in a pure difference.

In that place in the chain, there persists an equivalence between signifiers (as Lacan terms it in Seminar XI) that, losing their essential function, embody in the body the real of the letter without symbolic mediatization.

This equivalence between signifiers is equivalent to the value of the number in the experiment seen in Pavlov's conditioned reflex, where it operates as a pure frequency. The numerical frequency of the bells is what conditions the reflex, producing salivation even if the stimulus is not the food. In psychosomatic phenomena, the signifiers subtracted from their essential function and functioning only as equivalents between themselves, cause an induction that, as is the case in Pavlov's experiment, alters the biological function of the organism.

Lacan takes from linguistics the term holophrase to point out this specific modality in which signifying induction occurs. The holophrase indicates a weld in the first dyad of signifiers, between S1 and S2, which leaves no interval for the location of the subject in the experience of the discourse.

Thus, we warn that a patient's words that often appear as printed words, that remain circumscribed in their enunciation, full of meaning, and are little prone to become involved with associations, require an analytical listening to grant them a holophrase value.

I'll include a fragment of a clinical example to highlight some of these issues: Alberto, a 38-year-old patient, single. He comes to the office complaining of psoriasis that extends from his scalp, across his forehead, and down to his cheeks. He has visited several specialists and has conducted expensive treatments for years with no favorable results. Then, because of this, his last dermatologist suggested he get psychological treatment.

In the first interview he said with remarkable inaccuracy that the condition appeared about six years prior, when his parents finally separated after a coexistence plagued by fights and abuses.

This dermal injury had had long periods of remission. However, in the last couple of years, it had intensified by taking on a scaly and deep pink appearance that stretched across his *face*. He told how lately he had been able to observe that during the weekends it was exacerbated and accompanied by nasal colds, fever and physical exhaustion. "This leaves me disheartened. I have my hands tied, and I can't do my usual weekend activities, going out with friends, going for a run, or sailing."

His work activities were going pretty poorly. Some business opportunities that he set out on failed, and he *confronted* and fought with his clients needlessly. He had difficulty *addressing* work situations at a business that he had continued from his father.

The *discouragement*, or lack of encouragement, which he repeatedly used to describe his emotional status over the weekends, when his friends invited him to go out, became "I can't build up the courage" which led him to talk about his fears, about not knowing what to say when he went out with girls (the way his mother, a bit dismissively, referred to young women), especially when he was really attracted to one. Thus, the inhibition made him unable to utter a word.

Gradually, he began to take up again activities that he had abandoned and to go out with friends who he had distanced himself from during his sick spells.

On one occasion, he entered the session all grumpy saying that last Sunday he had gone sailing with some friends. He had been interested in one of the girls in the group, but nothing advanced at all. He added, "I couldn't face her," referring to being unable to ask her for her phone number.

Let's remember that these psoriatic spots spread down his *forehead* and face. That's why I asked him, if his being unable to *face* a girl that he likes is related to the spots on his face, and I asked for him to make associations with that word.

He said, "Facing someone is the same as confronting someone." He added that before his parents separated, he lived confronting his father. He described fights where they argued, and that even laid hands on each other. He was always *confronting* paternal anger, in the defense of a mother who always played the role of the victim.

He told that after those fights, he would feel miserable, exhausted, and weary, just like he felt now over the weekends or after some business venture in which he invested maximum effort and then failed.

It had been two years since his father had passed away. A frightening father who imposed himself through violence, generating situations of provocation and aggression, where the children took the side of defending a mother who they believed to be powerless. It was a paternal version that was inoperative for crossing out the maternal enjoyment. Alberto's younger brother, having been hospitalized several times, was diagnosed with paranoid schizophrenia.

There arises a way to work out the mourning of a father who he couldn't avoid. If one can only do without their father on the condition of making use of him, Alberto not only couldn't disregard his father but, despite being dead, and perhaps precisely because of this, he become huge and acquired a fierce consistency.

Face, confront: in associations the verbal form slips into an infinitive without a subject. We think of them as holophrases, an enunciative modality in which the S eludes being represented in the chain, without reaching significant value, as is the case of neurotic symptoms. In effect, they are embedded, while holophrases, in the real body (front and face).

Thus, it's through the avenue of analysis, the contingent path, through which something ceases to not be written, that a letter that lay encapsulated, muzzled in a specific materialized enjoyment of the libidinal stasis, begins to circulate in the chain, able to be read.

In this way, there were moments in the process of the treatment when the condition diminished and had almost become imperceptible. Some of these moments when some shift occurs in the economy of the enjoyment are more susceptible than others, which are to be understood as an effect of the analytical interventions.

Often, when the condition worsened, Alberto requested an increase in the number of sessions. This makes us think, as we said at the beginning, in a twist where what appeared muted as a phenomenon, scaling and coloring the forehead and face, goes about finding a way to reveal itself and revealed by a symptom in transit.

THE PAIN OF MOURNING

The theoretical constructions of the object *a* and the Borromean knot allow us to treat the concept of mourning as an insert to the specificity of a clinical method considered Lacanian. What type of mourning is treated in the course of an analysis? Undoubtedly, a fundamental one, the one that reaches the most inaccessible boundaries of castration, but without ignoring or, better yet, passing through the other mournings. Mourning for the absent loved object, mourning for the other sex, mourning for the murder of the father, mourning for the youthfulness of the body, mourning for what was not. Some people go through it with pain, a tear that hurts the body.

The Real Mourning: Pain in the Imaginary Body

It's right at the beginning of the Great War that Freud imprints the term "mourning" with psychoanalytic tradition in the famous text *Mourning and Melancholia*. It was a precursor, along with *Thoughts for the Times on War and Death* and *On Transience*, to the confection in 1920 of the concept of the death drive, a gear of repetition that determines the fate of a subject.

Mourning, in Freud's words, is regularly the reaction to the loss of a loved person, or to the loss of some abstraction which has taken the place of one, such as one's country, liberty, an ideal, and so on. The wise Freudian pen ends the series with the particle "and so on," which allows us to add elements. Why not add for today, for example, jobs, devoured by technology, suffers from increasing unemployment?

The term "mourning" exceeds singularity. Every age, every logos, every collective structure will have peculiar ways of dealing with the deaths of its men, its ideologies, and its ideals. Its various modes of expression will be a faithful reflection of the limits of the symbolic trauma to state the traumatic, always in excess.

Various conundrums run through the classic Freudian text. The proposal is to start from some of its theoretical cruxes and, in the light of the conceptualization of the object and the Borromean knot, reflect on melancholized mourning and the place assigned to the imaginary body as a receptacle of the pain of mourning.

What I would like to emphasize is that *Mourning and Melancholia* ends up alluding to an issue tangential to the one he addresses at the beginning about the difference between mourning and melancholia, but which I believe is precisely the key to dig deeper into the accentuation of the difference.

It's the one that, since *Draft G*, comes to form the core of the problem. It alludes to the painful nature of mourning. Briefly, we could formulate it like this: Why does mourning hurt? That painful wound, hemorrhage, the result of the breakage of associations, why does it hurt? Where does it hurt?

The mourning process is intimately connected to pain. Twofold are the pathways that cause it. If the representation of the lost object is kept invested, it suffers from not finding a sensory correlate. The longing for the object is not satisfied. On the other hand, the removal of the libido from an object that is no longer in itself produces pain since it requires the dismantling of a phantasmatic scaffolding that took time to build, and that is of a high degree of complexity.

Ten years later, in 1925, with the subject of anxiety as the background in *Inhibitions, Symptoms and Anxiety*, he raises the question once again and demands to differentiate mourning from pain. This led to inserting the body into a central role. Physical pain occurs in the real body. And so, we reformulate the question to try and approximate a conjecture: the pain of mourning, in what body does it hurt?

I propose to think that mourning hurts in the imaginary body.

Though we know that the notion of the body requires it being bound to the three registers—real, symbolic, and imaginary, Lacan, in *The Third*, a text in the final stages of its production, offers us a knot in which the body resides only the ring of the imaginary, life resides in the ring of the real, and death resides in the ring of the symbolic. In the center, where the three holes are covered, he places the object *a*. I think I can read into the placement of the body in the ring of the imaginary an attempt at a return to prioritizing this register in relation to what concerns the body. It isn't, as in the earlier seminaries, about the image of the body or an imaginary, merely specular body, but an imaginary body bound to the symbolic and the real. Depending on whether there was a joyful encounter with the image or not, a propitiatory tension is held between the object *a* and the *i(a)*.

The stabilization of the knot requires of the coordinate a subtraction of the object *a* in the R, S, and I.

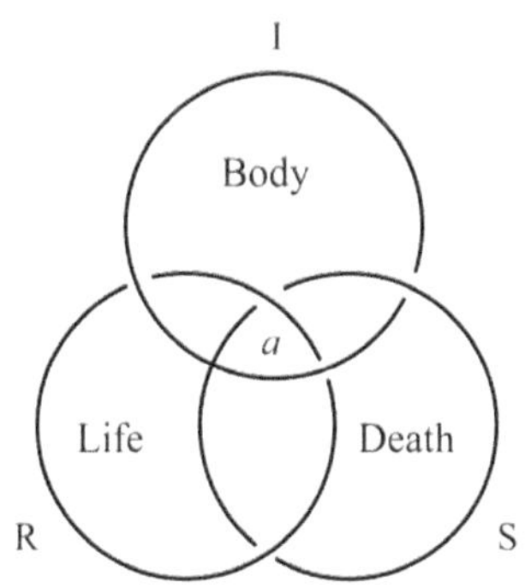

Figure 5.2 Body, Life, and Death in the Borromean Knot. *Source:* Created by the author.

This knot in which the body resides in the imaginary ring gives an account of a body in which the phallus is subtracted from the image. In the ring of the imaginary, what was subtracted in the object *a* takes on the identity of the negativized phallus, which grants shape and also jubilation to the mirror image. When the absence loses its location, the symbolic lack, this has an impact on the distortion that the mirror image i(*a*) suffers and the phenomena proper to melancholized mourning.

I propose, then, a reading of mourning through the Borromean knot.

A hole in the real, a loss in life that concerns existence. Existence, not with respect to the environment, but the one that reaches the most inner core, that which stirs the entire signifying universe. The symbolic order becomes disorganized and the lack loses its location. Generally, the subject doesn't find out how to take advantage of the new identity granted to them by an object that no longer has a correlate in reality. Affirming oneself as an orphan or widow means going through serious vicissitudes. Loss of localization of the lack, phantasmatic shaking. It's a pain in the imaginary body at the expense of the effacement of the lack in the Other, by intrusion, an impact of a plus on the mirror image. What's expected to be absolutely negativized, becomes positive: the imaginary phallus.

The weight of the object that punctures existence is consistent. It solidifies in the imaginary body. It mortifies it.

The Scene of a Comedy on the Tragedy of Mourning

As always, or as usually occurs, it's the analysts who induce us to write. They also lead us to read and write there where we read, and to invent there where the calligraphy becomes pale.

Let's then carry out a reading, a clinical reading, whose peculiarity was introduced in full dramatic fashion in a comedy: *The Imaginary Invalid* by Molière.

Cecilia, actress, thirty-five years old.

She introduces herself: "I've been in very bad shape for a year. Every day I cry. My face is disfigured by my crying. My partner mistreats me. He's crazy, and besides, he doesn't touch me. I have to ask him to please touch me." She continues, "My body always ends up reacting. My eye swells up, my leg hurts, I get a stomachache."

> Juan makes me suffer. He is just like my mom. I always had to be there, taking care of her. I got to the point where I wished she was dead. She died several years ago, but she still won't leave me alone even after she died. She said that more than loving me, she needed me. I'm always the victim.

Her mother had died the day Cecilia showed her the ticket that would realize a long-awaited dream of hers, visiting Europe.

She said, "She was sick all her life, complaining, whining. They never found anything wrong with her, but that day she fell asleep, and it was nerve-racking. I was with my sister, and we couldn't wake her up."

> She said that I had always been very independent. When I was born, she had postpartum depression for a month. She couldn't touch me, and then, when she got the courage to touch me, I would spit her breast out. They gave me a bottle.

I intervened, "She couldn't touch you. Looks like you found someone in Juan who you can persistently ask to touch you."

A concern over a work problem arises. A poster theme. She doesn't like the placing or the font they used for her name on the poster that will go on the theater marquee at the next premiere. She had never taken notice of such things, but now she was completely miffed. She approached the production manager to raise the issue, and, to her surprise, he acceded to her demands without objections, modifying the poster.

She related, "I went to ask him all broken down, in that style of complaint that characterizes me, always the poor thing, the victim. It seems to me that this costume is already becoming too small for me."

She associated it with a memory: "Some time ago I had to play the woman from *The Imaginary Invalid*, from Molière's comedy." She adds, "There was a scene that I couldn't get right."

> "My husband, the imaginary invalid, just like my mom, was playing dead. I had to shout, "How lucky you died, I'm finally going to be happy!" The director told me that I didn't get it right, that I lacked authenticity, that in that scene I didn't dazzle.

She asked herself, "Will I be able to be happy without being subject to someone to suffer? It looks like that scene isn't in me, I don't have it. . . . Will I just have to make it up?"

What isn't present, what wasn't reflected in the gaze of the Other, that place that didn't foster jubilation, is the place of maximum repetitive recidivism. It's accentuated *in extremis* in the mourning when in the face of the aggressor's death.

It's a paradoxical dynamic that triggers mourning. It brings the past to the present, crushing the object that, though mortifying, disappeared from the scene, returning as a shadow, perpetuating, and "melancholizing" the mourning.

I would like to propose some thoughts concerning the practice of the act of the analyst. Well removed from a clinical practice that proposed to recover and restore the lost objects, the one that we deal with alludes to the reencounter with the word but in the thickness of the letter. The letter is the instrument that bores through the enjoyment to register the absence. It's the scalpel with which the analyst's desire delicately operates.

In the first logical period of mourning, in which the denial dictates, it becomes necessary to name the loss, register it, recognize it, and place it within the structure to, from there, proceed to cut. As an imaginary agent, symbolic or real, the analyst intervenes, a midwife of the act.

Though the mourning may work, that doesn't always indicate that it serves a function, that is, that the loss was subjectivized, that the subject obtained the handwritten deed of the absence. Naming oneself in relation to the lost object is one of the ways of locating the absence. Sometimes, the language doesn't even provide the words to say it. Many other words will have to have the letters rearranged to bring about those names.

Cecilia was a face disfigured by tears, *the victim* of a mother who harassed her from birth, an imaginary invalid. The melancholic matrix bore notice of the vicissitudes in the constitution of the *i(a)*, the narcissistic image. Having come about death of the progenitor, the mourning was bogged down by the crushing nature of melancholy, without being able to cross over from pain to desire.

Recognizing that this disguise, this victim costume, was already too small for her, and that she preferred another attire, *better placement in the marquee*, put pressure on the crystallized place that repeatedly condemned her to play the victim in other relationships of love.

In an analysis, walking through the periods of mourning leads not to the mere substitution of one object with another, but to a certain access to the supplementary. It's a boosted enjoyment that forces an inscription and alters the logic of the chain in which it's registered. It's a real nomination that inaugurates the stroke with which a subject is reborn.

NOTES

1. Freud in *On Narcissism* defines erotogenicity: "Let us now, taking any part of the body, describe its activity of sending sexually exciting stimuli to the mind as its 'erotogenicity'" (Freud 1957a, 84).

2. I thank the Licentiate Viviana Dreidemie for her personal communication about this case.

BIBLIOGRAPHY

Freud, S. 1953. "Mourning and Melancholia" in *SE, Vol. XIV.*

Freud, S. 1953b. "Fragment of an Analysis of a Case of Hysteria" in *SE, Vol. VII.*

Freud, S. 1955. "Studies on Hysteria" in *SE, Vol. II.*

Freud, S. 1957a. "Mourning and Melancholia" in *SE, Vol. XIV*, 237–58.
Freud, S. 1957a. "On Narcissism" in *SE, Vol. XIV*, 67–104.
Freud, S. 1957a. "On Unconscious" in *SE, Vol. XIV*, 159–215.
Freud, S. 1959a. "Inhibitions, Symptoms and Anxiety," in *SE, Vol. XX*, 77–178.
Freud, S. 1964a. "Analysis Terminable and Interminable" in *SE, Vol. XXIII*, 209–53.
Freud, S. 1966. "Draft G. Melancholia (Undated. ? January 7, 1895)" in *SE, Vol. 1*, pp. 200–205
Lacan J. 1966. "La place de la psychanalysedans la médecine [The place of psychoanalysis in medicine]," *Cahier du College de Medicine,* 12: 761–74.
Lacan, J. 1978. *The Seminar of Jacques Lacan: The Four Fundamental Concepts of Psychoanalysis: Book XI*. New York: W.W. Norton & Company.
Lacan, J. 1989. "Geneva Lecture on the Symptom," *Analysis No. 1*. Melbourne: Centre for Psychoanalytic Research, 7–26.
Lacan, J. 2014. *Anxiety: the Seminar of Jacques Lacan, Book X*. Cambridge: Polity.

Chapter 6

Mourning and the Limit of the Structure

DISTORTIONS OF THE ACT IN HALTED MOURNING

In all likelihood, inhibition is the condition of the act most described and well-known to be a result of the state of mourning. Its manifestation compromises the execution of the act sparked by a desire up to the limit of its abolition, its annulment.[1] Generalized inhibition harasses those who are immersed in bereavement, as described by Freud in *Mourning and Melancholia.* A marked decrease of strength and energy accompanies the depressive state, which results in the thought process and even action being severely stunted. Nonetheless, we find that, as a result or manifestation of mourning halted or impeded in its times of elaboration, there are distortions of the act, phenomena such as repetitive acting out and *passage à l'acte*. They are modes of action that leave the subject lost with respect to the direction of their desire. The subject appears erratic, subordinated to a repetition compulsion that is not defined as neither good nor bad, but which is a failed attempt to register the trauma of the loss.

Next, we will deal with the issues of acting out and *passage à l'acte* as expressions of the vicissitudes in the processing of significantly traumatic mourning.

ACTING OUT: STATING THE UNSPEAKABLE

If I started from the title, maybe I should stick to a speech without words. However, and fortunately, as generally happens to analysts, the real that appears daily in practice makes us talk, to try to say what is impossible to say, what doesn't cease to not be written.

Relating in what circumstances it began and also some sequences of the analysis of Alcira that advance until a moment where the predominance of the action, the *agieren* or the acting out, gains ground over discursive deployment and threatens the continuation of the analysis.

Alcira called because she was worried about her son Mariano. She said she thought he needed treatment. I proposed scheduling an appointment to talk about it.

She said in this interview that Mariano is her eldest son. He was twelve years old. She was worried because:

> He is eating poorly. He always had problems with food, but now they got worse. I can't get him to eat a varied and complete diet. He is very thin. The only thing he likes to eat is pizza and all kinds of junk food, like cheese puffs, chips, when he goes to his friends' houses he makes sandwiches with mustard and mayonnaise.

She said it all started twenty months ago, when his sister was born.

> It was at that time that he stopped eating well. He even stopped eating solids. Also, he's always grumpy, he is constantly aggravating and starting fights with his sisters, who are 10 and 8 years old respectively. He has problems with everything. Sometimes we are calm, and he arrives and everything becomes chaotic.

During these years they consulted with pediatricians who prescribed vitamins, but as far as Alcira knew, they were more to please her than to give the child what he actually required.

When I asked her what Mariano's father thinks of her request for treatment for their son, she told me that she divorced him when the youngest daughter was four months old. Two years after the death of her mother, whom he had always held responsible for Mariano's eating problems. She said that as a father he was always "insufficient." Compared to the attention he gave to the daughter of his second marriage, she said that these children are like second-class citizens. He didn't see it as necessary that Mariano get treatment, but he agreed to pay for it like other activities his children did.

At some point during the interview, and related to her concern that Mariano didn't eat solids (she would get distressed and feed him anything; it's what her husband reproached her about), she said that they had lost a-year-and-a-half-old son in an accident. He drowned when the sailboat in which they were sailing was shipwrecked. (Immediately after the accident, she became pregnant with Mariano.) Before some questions of mine, she clarified that she preferred not to talk about it, that it was something very painful, that it was already in the past, that she believed that it didn't have much to do with the consultation and insistently requested that I see Mariano.

Then the consultations with Mariano began, who was somewhere between quiet and annoyed to have to come.

He referred to his sisters who continually bothered him, and he made a drawing that he described in this way: "It's a carnivorous plant that spits seeds and plants grow. With one of its tentacles it grabbed a guy by his foot. It's like the Family Game" (TN: In Latin America, the home video games were called "Family Game").

Next to this figure that was like a jellyfish with a huge mouth and several tentacles, the longest of which was tied to the ankle of one foot, he drew a sign, and on it a skull with two crossed bones as a symbol of death.

I saw Mariano just a few times, because he was reluctant to come to the session, since it had become another obligation for him, imposed by his mother, such as going to piano or English classes. Alcira began to make repeated calls where she complained and in anguish asked what she should do. In view of this, I implied that it wasn't Mariano who seemed to need something to change; she did.

A few days later she called to request an appointment. From there followed some interviews that became an analysis currently in progress.

Sometime later I remarked that this drawing, with the words that went with it in Mariano's description, represented the place Mariano kept in relation to the "carnivorous plant of his family game." He described how the death of his brother had affected him before his birth, in that sailboat accident of which his mother had not been able to speak about or process in the least, not even the bare minimum for an event of such magnitude that can be processed so that it doesn't end up, among other things, having such a threatening or detrimental impact on her other children.

During one of the first moments of analysis, it became clear that who she called an "insufficient father" for her children, even though he seemed to be attentive and present for their needs, actually had been insufficient in saving her son Darío in the accident that they had.

But in her own story, what father had been insufficient? Remembering the tragedy about the loss of her son sent her to another previous tragedy. She remembered her mother fleeing their home when she was four years old with her two-year-old brother after a strong fight between her parents. She has a blurry image in her mind of her father going to the kitchen and grabbing a knife.

A short time later, the father stole her brother when school let out. From then on a paternal version was forged through her mother saying that this extended to all men. "All of them are cowards, inconsistent, lazy, insufficient. They abandon women." Her mother did nothing to recover her son, and since then the encounters between them (with her father and brother) were very sporadic.

Evidently, Mariano, as a male child, and to the extent that he is becoming a man, becomes one more element in this series.

Regarding her ex-husband, with whom she had formed an employee-owned company—both are quite successful professionals in their careers—she said,

> Although I felt that when I got married I was very much in love, and having to face my mother who told me that same day that she felt that I was killing her with my marriage. Suddenly [they separated two years after the death of her mother], I felt that my husband was an obstacle that didn't let me grow, expand. He belittled me, that's why I got divorced. I wanted to try my luck without being subservient to him.

Alcira talked about how "faithful" she was to her mother during her childhood. When I asked about this, she revealed that, among other things, she was faithful to her by not denying anything when she introduced herself as a widow, and Alcira as an orphan.

Mourning for the death of her son sent her to a previous mourning, for the absence of a father, who according to maternal speech had to be considered dead, allying a mother and daughter in a lie that made them a fictional orphan and widow.

During an early stretch, the scene of analysis chiefly passed remembering that first child, the accident, and the burial, often accompanied by a continuous and silent crying.

She told how this baby was nicknamed *Smiles* because he was always smiling, well fed, chubby, and in a good mood. With this abrupt loss, she had been at an irreducible point of idealization, compared to Mariano who quickly came to occupy an impossible place, bringing together all the opposite qualities.

On one occasion, she said that after the accident she clung to her husband. She wanted him to repair the loss. A month after the accident, she became pregnant with Mariano and then, shortly thereafter, pregnant with her two daughters (let's remember the description of the drawing: a carnivorous plant that spits seeds).

She subsequently began to wonder about her father. A memory surfaced: once when her father had visited her, in her childhood, he brought her some cookware as a gift, which she loved, but her mother decided to share it with a cousin of hers. She said, "From a whole set, I only had a few pieces left."

In recent times, she had strengthened her ties with her brother, which resulted in some proximity to her father. It was an attempt to go find her own version of those who were missing from her story and bring back said family ties.

She started to not be so distressed with Mariano's behavior and eating habits. It's no longer a central issue. She was finally able to materialize some reforms to make her home nicer, something she had desired for a long time. She mentioned the kindness of one of her neighbors, who despite the inconvenience that it could cause him, allowed her to carry out the renovation and expand her house.

This coincided with a period in which she began to worry about her body, about a few extra pounds, which she said made her a friendly fatty. "I can't lose weight, even though I try different diets." "I spend time being careful with my meals, but then night comes, and I can't. Yesterday I ate six alfajores."

That is when a period of turbulence began in the analysis: requests for continuous schedule changes, late arrivals, attacks on the device (she would arrive and sit in a chair instead of lying on the couch), and, full of anxiety, insisting on saying that she wanted to leave, that she didn't want to keep coming.

This period, characterized by forms of acting, in which it is difficult to maneuver the transference, and in which the continuation of analysis is threatened, has in its entirety an aspect of resistance. Nonetheless, I also thought that, being a call to interpretation, it's a privileged phenomenon so that they enter the path where situations of loss in the real are processed, and I deliberately did not say elaborated (*durcharbeiten*).

Let's go back to the beginning of this journey, and from there try to locate this moment in which a scene, that of acting out, is mounted on the scene of the device.

Alcira consulted distressed by her son, when he was entering adolescence. At the precise time when he is no longer a child and is becoming a man. It was the moment of separation that revived an unhealed wound, the death of a child in his early infancy. This, in turn, led her to go through other losses in her story.

Up to a certain point, where her own body appeared as an obstacle to the continuation of the analysis, she started talking about those extra kilos, that excess weight that she couldn't lose despite going on the most varied diets. She was able to control herself all day, but at night, compulsively, she ate six alfajores.

This stretch of analysis was accompanied by continuous calls to change the session schedule, late arrivals, and an interruption announcement, in which she said she didn't want to keep talking, since that wouldn't make her lose weight. All until she could finally say, "I am like the tower of Pisa. I read that when the axis doesn't pass through the center of the body, it'll collapse."

It was a phrase enunciated *a posteriori* of the acting, but in serious relation with it, and that allowed for an interpretation to be made and I told her: "The one who eats pizza is Mariano. How scary would it be that that stop being the axis!"

After this, new associations took place, and she could continue to talk about her body beyond her children's bodies. It opened the doors for her to talk about her femininity beyond the perspectives of motherhood.

From the dawn of psychoanalysis, Freud warned that in the course of analysis there is a phenomenon that takes place and prevents remembrance, in which resistance occupies the transference dimension, and sometimes it can threaten the continuation of the analysis. To speak of this phenomenon, he used the term *agieren*, which translated to English is acting out. As such, and in a sort of impossibility of translation that comes with its definition, it passed through analytical literature to the present day.

I was interested in underlining the coincidence between *agieren* (act) and *abreagieren* (abreact) to support the hypothesis that acting out is not only resistance, as it was considered for a long time, but also an inescapable moment of healing. Especially when it comes to elaborating mourning. The structure of acting out lends itself so that the work of mourning, in its constant movement to recover the loved object, and in turn recognize it as lost, enter paths of processing.

In *Remembering, Repeating and Working-Through*, Freud introduced the term "compulsion to repeat" to refer in the transference to what is not repeated through remembrance. It could be said, then, that the repetition in the analysis is carried out along the route of memory, a signifying route, which is a repetition that always involves a loss—it's a constitutive repetition of the subject, since it gives rise to interpretation so that in its function of cutting, it produces the fall of the object—or by the route of compulsion, which would be more apt to call reproduction than repetition, as Freud does in *Beyond the Pleasure Principle*, or automatism as designated by Lacan, clearly referring to the staging. This mode does not bring the loss into play, nor is it in the series of demands as the term re-petition indicates, but, rather, in calling to the Other. This act, this automatism, or acting out, is a call to interpretation, but without giving it space during its staging, because during the course we don't have the materiality of the speech. I would say that the interpretation is not viable until a later time, an *aprés-coup* moment, in which that scene, mounted onto the analysis scene, can retroactively enter the associative chain.

In the Seminar X, *Anxiety* (1962–1963), Lacan, where during the whole seminar he had placed acting out in the table, in the last class, replaced it with mourning. What role would acting out have in relation to the work of mourning?

If to love is to give what one does not have, the loved object constitutes the support of the lack. With the loss in the real of the object of love, the object of the lack, which the subject located in the Other, is thrown at the subject. Therefore, the controversial concept of acting out would be an attempt to register an absence, in the place where the real loss of the loved object updates it the way most replete of meaning. Although it appears threatening to rupture the device, the subject doesn't want to detach themselves from the analysis, but from the object that in mourning presents itself in an unyielding way.[2] Acting out is the scene that mounts the desire to provoke and to attempt the fall of the object, and thus allow to process something of the mourning.

Acting is making the object present, the automatism of the object. Called to interpretation, but not giving it space, since in its anticipation, in its attempt to avoid anguish, both the subject and the signifiers that determine it are left out.

We know, since Freud, that a son comes to solve an equation for a woman. Though neurosis doesn't cease to demonstrate that she fortunately doesn't achieve it, I believe that this equation is not only symbolic, but also corresponds to the real, to the real of the immediacy of the bodies that makes the maternal filiation. Every pregnancy leaves a mark on the body.

Could a mourning be elaborated for the death of a child?

Perhaps we can say that it's unthinkable since there's no word in the language for it. What do we call a mother if her child dies? You cannot say orphan or widow. There's no word that names that case of loss, played out in the real of her body.

Passage à L'Acte: Notes on Suicide

In May 1998, public opinion was shaken by the news of a suicide. It was a suicide that closed the chapter on speculations on the whereabouts of the businessman wanted by the law,[3] the protagonist of this story, and opened new chapters on endless conjectures that would give meaning to this unusual and unexpected act. Suicide, an untimely and exaggerated departure from the scene of the world, always causes a certain amount of wonder, surprise, and intrigue. What are the motives that make someone decide to interrupt their existence? What causes a subject to pull the trigger on his temple, or to go through the window frame and throw himself, to ingest a lethal dose of psychotropic drugs, or to lacerate his body with a real and deadly cut? This act borders the limit of rationality.

Suicide would seem to be the only alternative to the corralling of what's irremediable, to a game lost beforehand, without even admitting the possibility of a chance that subverts the predicted destiny.

Frequently, by the notes found or by what families and relatives say, it wouldn't be strange to think, considering the peculiarity of each case, that, for the suicidal person, all the roads lead to a critical crossroads, in which death is the only possible way out.

Lacan specified the notion of *passage à l'acte*, used to designate impulsive forms of acting, and that in Freud is homologized to the term of Latin origin *agieren*, which he uses to refer to different ways of a hurried, seized action.

These impulsive modes of action leave the subject expelled from the world scene, falling precipitously from the phantasmatic frame. There are several ways that a *passage à l'acte* can show its face, however, suicide is surely its extreme expression. In the seminar *Anxiety*, we find the following statement:

> The moment of the *passage à l'acte* is the moment of the subject's greatest *embarrassment*, with the behavioural addition of *emotion* as a disorder of movement. It is then that, from where he is—namely, the locus of the stage where alone, as a fundamentally historicized subject, he is able to maintain himself in his status of subject—he rushes and topples off the stage, out of the scene. This is the very structure of the *passage à l'acte*. (Lacan 2014, 115)

From its beginnings, psychoanalysis dealt with this subject. Let's remember Dora's father's concern about the letter written by his daughter, in which she said goodbye forever, claiming that she could not endure life any longer, or the eloquent attempt of the young homosexual woman to throw herself onto the tracks where the streetcar passed.

This is a recurring theme for analysts, coming from different angles, which shows up in different versions. Sometimes, it comes in the form of one or several suicide attempts, that is, when the consultation is caused by a foiled attempt to end their lives. Other times it's because the whole course of an analysis is about the insistence on the question of what led a parent to commit that act. On other occasions, it's because the analysis begins to pass through an "area" plagued by acting outs, and in which, if the analytical process via interpretation doesn't take place, it could lead to a *passage à l'acte*.

I remember the case of the children of an older lady who were very worried and consulted me because when they visited her mother, they found her in a severe coma. She had ingested a high dose of sleeping pills, the prey of an acute state of confusion. What this woman later related was that a watch supplier which she had known for many years had gone to her business—the watchmaking store she had taken over after the death of her husband, which had recently occurred. When this man left, she was certain that "she lacked many important pieces." On her way home, she became distraught and swallowed all the pills in the bottle on her table. She began to tell that in a few days it would be her birthday, the first she would celebrate without her partner of so many years. She told how lonely and lost she felt in her own house without his presence, and clarified, "at night I'm afraid. I feel cold. He always covered me." He had been the watchmaker, somehow the one who repaired the watches, the one that marked her times. His sudden death had left her without a phantasmatic cover, without someone who would "cover" her, misplacing watches, lost in time.

Suicide, or its attempt, as the maximum expression of *passage à l'acte*, an untimely impulse to leave the world scene, is a consequence of the driven defusion, since it was the object now lost on which the libidinal tension and the drive ligature fell. The death drive, now untied, falls on the ego. In melancholic structures faced with traumatic bereavements, suicide attempts are often found. The narcissistic wound caused by the loss of the object is like a libidinal hemorrhage that causes a subjective abolition. In the attempt to deny the loss of the object, by alienation—I think it exceeds an identification—from it, the subject faces their own destiny, throwing themselves from the scene of life to the waters of death.

Let's look at the account a young woman makes of the *passage à l'acte* that she led shortly after her mother's suicide.

Olga arrived at the consultation extremely sorrowful. She reported that a year ago she returned from the United States with a six-year-old son. She said, "I am going through a very harsh and depressive slump. I came back because my brothers told me that I was going to be much better here, and this is a disaster."

Very depressed, she mentioned fragments of her family history in the first interviews. The only daughter of four brothers, her father, a senior military officer, died of a rampant cancer when she was a teenager and her mother, a woman with a long history of psychiatric treatment, had an "accident"—in the words of the patient—wanting to jump from one balcony to another to escape to buy alcohol, she died falling into the gap. It just so happens that it was Olga's turn to take care of her in the schedule that her family had organized.

She clearly remembered the accusations made at her mother's funeral by the maternal grandmother, who was shouting "killer." Exhausted from looking after her so that she didn't commit a suicide with pills and alcohol, she wanted to sleep for a while and decided to lock the mother in the bedroom where she threw herself. When she woke up the police and firemen had shown up, "it was hell."

Shortly after starting the treatment, she entered the session with a noticeable scratch on her nose. She told me that she didn't know how it happened, that she had been talking to a friend of her ex-partner, the father of her son, who left when she was three months pregnant, and that she was so angry that at night, while sleeping, she accidentally hurt herself.

I asked her if she always hurt herself, apparently without even realizing it, when she got upset and angry. She replied that she doesn't know how she did it either, but that a year after her mother's death, she shot herself and pointed at the center of her diaphragm. "The doctor said it was a miracle that I was alive. It was one millimeter off of hitting the aorta, and a centimeter off of hitting the spine. It came out from behind. They had to perform surgery on me."

I asked her to detail what happened immediately after her mother's death. She remembered that she became seriously ill, bruises started appearing on her arms, lots of nosebleeds, one of her fingers became paralyzed, she thought she had leukemia, she was hospitalized for a month, then she gave in and returned home.

> I didn't tell you because you were going to think that I needed to be interned, but some grim things happened in my house. When I wasn't there, someone would come into my room, scramble up my drawers, open the closet doors, and turn on the lights. One day when a friend stayed over to sleep, she also heard noises in my room, and we were the only ones in the house. I would get desperate. I think that's how one day, I saw the key to the safe where my brothers kept their weapons, grabbed it, then let it go, many times until I opened it and shot myself.

There had been a lapsus in this story, which I simply interrogated but did not interpret, when she quickly recounted the treatments she was given during hospitalization. She made a mistake and said, instead of "they gave me transfusions," "they gave me anemia." A signifying lapsus that summarized her permanent complaint of not having been sufficiently loved by her parents, who preferred her male brothers. A lapsus that suggests the question of what family legacy she received as a woman. Olga repeated that her father had regret on his deathbed and said, "How he hadn't been able to see the daughter he had" as a posthumous recognition of the young woman.

That there is no grieving function means that the object *a* does not work in the structure. In the class on July 3, 1963, Lacan proposed that by structure, and according to how the gaze works as an object in the imaginary constitution of the ego, the subject may travel through life in the mourning-desire or melancholia-mania cycles. If there is a function of *a*, that is, the object *a* operating from lack of knowledge, but operating nonetheless, the subject may enter the mourning-desire cycle. If this doesn't happen, they enter into the mania-melancholia cycle. Here there is no function of *a* in the structure. Is there a foreclosure of the object *a*?

This would imply a logic of interventions that point to the creation of the object *a*, to create the status of the object *a* in the structure. These interventions are frequently done from the imaginary or the real. The analyst, with their presence, with their countenance and with their speech, will assist in the construction of the object. That the object works will encourage the phantasm to be constituted as a support of desire.

Taking this operation to an extreme, we can say that, if there is phantasmatic recomposition in the bereavement, the grim phantasms and apparitions stop swarming, strange phenomena—of the *Unheimlich*—typical of when a mourning is prevented from starting its elaboration.

In *Mourning and Melancholia*, Freud links the impulses of suicide to homicidal impulses, that is, originally oriented toward some libidinal object and then turned against the ego, directing itself toward it, hoisting it up as an object, with all the aggressive and hostile charge. He places the problem, then, at the level of narcissism. He points out that, in both suicide and extreme infatuation—opposite situations—the ego is equally dominated by the object. This is what Lacan takes up at the last session of the seminar *Anxiety*, when to mark the radical difference between melancholia and mourning, he warned that in the former, the object is the one that triumphs. Conducted to the terms of the algorithm of the phantasm, it's the object that commands the action in a setting where the subject is abolished. The suicidal person that throws themselves through the opening of a window seems to be the fullest expression of subjective suppression. It reflects the expulsion of the subject under the domain of the object.

We agree that generally when we refer to suicide—whether it was successful or an attempt—we link it with the *passage à l'acte*, as an escape, as an untimely exit from the scene to the pure world. It's an extreme act of annulment of the traces of subjectivation, disengagement of the symbolic plot, a driven diffusion that undresses a death drive that manifests itself as a destructive drive. As a *passage à l'acte*, suicide frequently occurs in the realm of melancholy, when the position of the subject is meager and identified with a cursed object.[4]

Walter Benjamin: A Man in Dark Times

However, sometimes, suicide seems to be a mode of response of the subject, a desperate attempt to restore an abolished dignity. It's the final resource in an attempt to historicize themselves against the annihilation of the traces of being human, in the face of genocide and the abuse of subjectivity. Juan Gelman made a similar reflection related to the death of the writer Virginia Woolf, who in May 1941 killed herself by throwing herself into the waters of the River Ouse. Shortly before she died, referring to how devastating the war was, she had written: "I could just see a piece of my studio wall standing: otherwise rubble where I wrote so many books." We believe that this is what Lacan refers to when, in the seminar XV, *The Psychoanalytic Act* (1967–1968), he attributes the act of suicide the exclusivity of an achievement, since there is none like it. In the seven talks at Sainte-Anne (1971–1972) called "The Knowledge of the Psychoanalyst" Lacan says, "We know that there is no act except a failed one and that it is even the only condition of a semblance of success. This indeed is why suicide deserves to be objected to" (Lacan 1971–1972, I9).

Suicide, in these cases, seems like a mode of reregistration in the generational chain, of reinstating the proper name against the imminent genocidal condemnation of anonymous disappearance, of extermination. This is the case of the suicide of the writer, essayist, and poet Walter Benjamin. It was a suicide with which he crossed the border between life and death, after the occupying forces closed the borders of Spain and his path to freedom to send him back to the concentration camps.

I'm interested in underlining some questions about this thinker and the outcome of his life, which I find offers the possibility of placing suicide as a subject's strategy before a real, devastating, and fierce Other.

Faced with Nazi persecution in Germany, from 1933 Benjamin had chosen to live in Paris. His place of work was the National Library, from where he continued writing for magazines and newspapers of the time.

In 1939, all German immigrants residing in France, by a decree from the German government, were designated as "stateless citizens," arrested, and sent to concentration camps. Benjamin was sent to the Nevers concentration camp. Soon he was released and undertook a trip to southern France, which was still free from Nazi occupation, along with other refugees.

In the letters of this era he showed unease and skepticism that refugees could escape the trap they were in as they roamed Europe fleeing from the shadow of the Holocaust, plunged into uncertainty, but he also showed his terrible dismay by finding himself, for the first time in his life "totally deprived of his books."

In September 1940, he had been granted a visa with which he could travel to Spain, and from there immigrate to America. But at the French border he was denied permission to leave France. Therefore, along with other refugees, and fleeing from the border police, they undertook crossing through the Pyrenees, arriving at Port-Bou, the first Spanish city. There they begged for their documents to be stamped to be able to enter Spain, but since they were "stateless citizens," and a recent Spanish decree forbade such people from traveling in their country, they announced that they would be escorted back to France the next morning. This meant the return to a concentration camp, degradation, torture, and extradition.

Faced with this ominous panorama, Benjamin, that same night, took his own life by consuming the morphine tablets he planned to ingest if he was captured.

Several years before, in 1915, Freud, when he worked on the topic of mourning, and it became a heritage of psychoanalytic language, had the insight to open a wide range of circumstances for which someone may mourn.

Thereby, he mentioned, of course, the loss of the loved person, but also one's country, liberty, or ideal.

According to some of his biographers, for Benjamin, who had loved and written so much about the Berlin of his childhood, exile had already been a hard blow.

In addition, as Hannah Arendt recounts in *Men in Dark Times*, trying to answer for said final act of taking his own life: "There were various reasons for this. The Gestapo had confiscated his Paris apartment, which contained his library and many of his manuscripts." She asks herself, "How was he to live without a library, how could he earn a living without the extensive collection of quotations and excerpts among his manuscripts?" (Arendt 1968, 170).

The cancellation of life on one's own account always produces questions.

In the clinic study of melancholia, the *passage à l'acte* is that suicidal action that leads unexpectedly to the exit of the world scene in a desperate attempt to effect separation with the object.

It's a martyrizing object that overshadows the subject, a submission to an Other who, embodied in the superego with fierce cruelty, demands a sacrifice.

In opposition to this, particularly in this case of the suicide of W. Benjamin, like others that occurred under circumstances of extreme human annihilation, it makes us question whether said act comes to the place of an accomplished act. Terminated, in the broadest sense of the term, only capable of restoring there the subject that pronounces, through said act, the decision-making regarding the dignity of their life.

Freud innovatively proposed, in 1915, the need for a work for mourning and logical times for its elaboration. This is not too far removed from the dark moments that loomed because of the war. It was a historical time in which man's conception in the face of death changed completely.[5]

Speaking of men in dark times, there were some very bleak sufferings in the century that has just passed, the twentieth, some more distant, others closer. I would like, then, to quote some allusive verses that W. Benjamin wrote upon the death of a friend who was a poet, Fritz Heinle, during the World War I in 1915:

On such a night, sleep is very rare
For the insomniac, it makes his clarity that could not
be of use for man during the day a gift,
But it turns its ray on his true worlds
No other light will bloom upon his threshold
Memory his moon and his comrade. (Benjamin 1993, 43)[6]

To conclude, at the dawn of another century and almost at the other end of the planet, may it be that we analysts retake that term—mourning—to which

Freud imprinted psychoanalytic heritage, and that through it, we delve into the annihilations of humanity and in the serious consequences of impeded and halted mourning. It is an ethical stake, especially when oblivion stalks and impunity threatens.

On Borders, Frontiers, Littorals: Thoughts on the Limit

The name of the present Conference "Limits of Treatments, Limitations of Therapists,"[7] within the framework of clinical practice, led me to think once more on the illnesses that afflict those who consult us. It's often a clinic field that has been called in different ways by its characteristics. They're ways that separate us from the Freudian tripartition—neurosis, psychosis, perversion—that Lacan later maintained. Some of these new denominations are: "borderline personality disorder," "narcissistic personality disorders," or, sometimes trying to locate it in an already known nosology, it's returned to archived terms long ago as it is the case of calling them "borderline pathologies." In recent years, there has been a push for the emergence of a multiple number of specialists for its treatment, in bulimia and anorexia, in addictions, panic attacks, and so on.

It's quite different from what we traditionally know as neurosis, including difficulties to install a neurosis of transference in the device, that is, that the symptom become in tune with the analyst, calling the unconscious into question. Now there are fewer consultations that revolve around affective disorders or existential problems worthy of a traditional neurosis, where inhibitions, symptoms, and anguish sting and interrogate the subject. It doesn't take on the characteristics of the conversive paralyses of the end of the nineteenth century in the manner of Elisabeth von R., or the tormenting doubts of Rat Man. In its place, in this presentation of neurosis, and almost contrarily at the end of the century, we frequently find an excessive and impulsive drive that characterizes the suffering of the age. It's what's characteristic of addictions to food and to not eating—as in bulimia and anorexia—of addiction to psychoactive drugs, alcohol, drugs, aesthetic surgeries. And also to the staging—read repetitive acting out—acting out, not as an isolated event, but as a constellation. It comes as a permanent action that leaves out the subject of desire, of the signifier and that in a chain can end up resulting in a *passage à l'acte*. Let's not fail to mention that said loosened action of desire contrasts and alternates frequently with crushing inhibitions in which overflowing anguish becomes panic.

Today, where the symptom—the privileged formation of the unconscious to state the suffering—frequently shows up without its formal envelope, but rather appears as unwrapped and embodied, in a continuous sacrificial offering of the body, interrogating the symptom to the brink imposes an approximation of the horizons of the clinical studies to the subjectivity of the time.

I will relate a clinical case that I think describes some of the aforementioned issues.

María, in the first interview, said,

> I came because I don't know where I am. I feel very bad. I started college. It's what I wanted, and now I don't go to classes. I'm scared. I stay at home. The other day a high school classmate called me to meet up, and I told her I couldn't. I made up an excuse. I didn't want to meet up. I'm 27 years old and I feel like I'm 17. I'm always in the same place, but with less desire and less of a chance of doing what I was presumably supposed to do. When she called me after not having seen each other for such a long time, the first thing I thought was that I'm the same as when I left high school. . . . In August of last year, I appeared in Rio de Janeiro, even today I don't understand how it happened. I wanted to leave my house, my boyfriend, the therapy. I wanted to leave my life. I worked in a law office with two lawyers who were brothers. I was the secretary of one who had been in a serious car accident and was hospitalized. He asked me to take some money from the bank the next day to collect my salary and pay the employees from the office. I got up the next morning and did what he had asked me, but I didn't go to the office. I started wandering the streets. I felt very cold. I felt the cold seep under my skin even though I was wearing a lot of layers. I was very stressed and felt that I couldn't breathe. Downtown was a compact and dark mass. That's how I got to where you can buy tickets for Brazil. I don't remember well how, but I arrived at the airport. I stayed in Rio for a while at a friend's house . . . and then I called, and they came to pick me up.

It would be very lengthy to thoroughly develop the different moments of this story. Starting with a reconstruction, during different sessions she began assembling and recovering that month and a half that she was in Rio, and of which in the first interviews she said she had no record of, as if an intense amnesia was at work there. However, she did remember in detail the scene of the day before she went away. She had gone to visit her boss, the lawyer from the office with whom she later revealed to have maintained an affectionate, sentimental relationship, at the hospital. She said that when she entered the room, she found her colleague, the other secretary, sitting on the bed in a suspiciously loving manner next to him.

She also remembered that her therapist, from whom she had hidden her sentimental relationships, seeing her one day very anxious and with severe headaches that made it feel like her head would explode, had uttered, "Don't worry, I am going to turn you into a normal person."

Maria had been yearning for a long time to begin studying for a Bachelor's of Art, which she had been systematically postponing for a few years. It had taken her ages to complete the Gen Ed, and when she came for consultation, it was because she liked the subjects she was enrolled in. But when she was about to leave for class, she would stay at home going round in circles. Sometimes she would say she was afraid to go outside. "I panic. It's like I'd like to go unnoticed. If I say something in class and they look at me, it makes me want to run away."

Some of the signifiers that gained prominence in the months of treatment were *nomadic* when she referred to her father. Since her childhood he traveled constantly and was absent from home for several days at a time since he was in charge of transporting newspapers and magazines in his truck to the countryside. Another one was *powerful* to refer to her mother. She was in charge at home. She is like the typical German woman: very energetic, strong, but she was always distant, so "I thought she didn't love me, and when she gave me a kiss it was a big event."

She dedicated herself enthusiastically to photography, and even though several of her photos had been published in different print media, she couldn't find a way to get paid for it. She described a phenomenon that occurred to her (I think it had the status of a visual hallucination), which she called the one in the image of "retinal persistence." She described it like this, "I have something in my eye that is shaking. I think that when there is a flash of light in my eyes, letters start to move for me. The letters tremble."

María is a constant reader. Session after session she came accompanied by a book that, as soon as she entered, she would rest on the desk between us. Italo Calvino and Carver are some of the authors who accompanied her. Last time she had one entitled *The X Generation.* She related, "This weekend my boyfriend and I were both lying in bed doing nothing. We're from this generation" and pointed at the book. In light of my questioning expression, she answered, "Slackers, Generation X, people who go through life without aspirations (outsiders). Their main activity is doing nothing. To watch TV, listen to rock, not produce anything. They come from the Nirvana generation. It's part of my common language."

In one of the last sessions, and referring to the oscillation of her activity as a photographer, which she had recently become more of a profession, she said, "I need to find a position in the middle. I go from omnipotence to a feeling of finding myself empty and lost."

Taking up the title of the work, it was in my interest to define some terms that are of service in practice that concern us for the purposes of diagnostic distinctions, and that therefore give the key—in the musical sense—to tune the instrument. I mean that they make sense for the direction of a cure, and basically not to go astray in an infinite nosology.

Usually, it's referred to as borderline disorder, for the case shown, which is exhibited on the stage instead of expressed through words. In it, the condition seems to be more defined as a phenomenon than a symptom. With a modality of repetitive actings, addictions, psychosomatic phenomena, and so on. Calling it, then, a borderline, the border of neurosis, would it not be avail to think that today neurosis is presented from its borders? That this is the mark on the selvedge that characterizes neurosis today?

So what do we mean when we say border? In topology, a discipline that studies the qualitative properties of figures and that, since Lacan introduced it, is not alien to the practice of psychoanalysis, the rim is what results in a surface caused by a cut, by a line called the edge. That is, the edge indicates that there has been a cut, but also that there has been a trace, a mark, a stroke of where to cut.

Lacan uses the term "rim phenomenon" to refer to anxiety in the class on January 23, 1963, in the seminar that dealt with this subject. He said,

> Freud's ultimate thinking points out that anxiety is a signal in the ego . . . a rim phenomenon in the imaginary field of the ego. The term rim derives its legitimacy from the affirmation by Freud himself that the ego is a surface and even, he adds, a surface projection. (Lacan 2014, 117)

In that same session he introduced, in relation to anxiety, the concepts of acting out and *passage à l'acte*. They're two topics that, regarding the clinic practice that concerns us today, send us back to think about the structure of neurosis with respect to the border, to the rim phenomenon.

In this seminar, based on the topological figure of the projective plane, he defined the relationship of the subject with the object, that is, the position of the subject in the phantom. We won't get into this but simply point out that the immersion of the projective plane in space results in the cross-cap. In other words, it results in a Moebius strip that represents the subject, and a disc that represents the object. The projective plane is the structure in which the place where the object is missing is marked. The structure is a projective plane in which the cut line separates the subject from the object. There is a point of intersection that is common to the band and the disc, but it's necessary that it be on the side of the disc, that is, what for us is the object. This point is called the singular point or hole-point. It is a point of concession to singularity. It seems to contain the unique feature that in the object is taken from the subject. There resides the cause that animates the subject of desire.

When we talk about the border, we're talking about the place in the structure where the object is missing, the emergence of the rim phenomenon, as Lacan calls anxiety, a sign in the ego of phantasmatic hesitation. There the phantom doesn't work as an imaginary coverage. There, in that area of the acting out relationship, the one that is out of the action is the subject.

I proposed the preceding route to affirm that the border is the efficacy of the marks that delimit the structure. They're marks that, in the instituting moments—alienation, separation—speak of the way in which castration operates.

The border makes the order of the letter. If through the signifier we proceed to the cut, the letter is what delimits the border. The underlying question might be: What relationship would there be between a signifier and a letter?

Lacan works through this question in a 1974 essay called "Lituraterre," announcing that the letter, particularly the one bearing the signifiers written in a letter, is not homogeneous with the message. The letter, written letter, is irreducible to the signifier.

As was attempted in psychiatric nosology, homologizing borderline with frontier doesn't keep theoretical rigor. The dictionary term that we'll work with for frontier is the confines of a State. In general, it's conventionally established on some notable geographical element of the land. It's established based on something that precedes it, which is why it isn't instituting, as the border is.[8] It's susceptible to modifications and all kinds of imaginary slippage that would limit a subject (under the binding labels of personality traits, character traits, or borderline personality).

The title says, "On Borders, Frontiers, Littorals." A littoral is what marks the border between heterogeneous spaces. Colloquially, it's synonymous with shore or coast. Thus, while the frontier is conventionally located between homologous territories, the border is littoral between heterogeneous spaces, such as knowledge, unconscious knowledge, and enjoyment in its grammar of drive.

Then, that which acts as a border in the structure is a littoral between the desire to know, typical of those who turn to an analyst, and that which, if they wish to know, they must be willing to renounce: we call it excess enjoyment.

The illnesses that presently show up have the characteristics of phenomena (I could mention descriptive phenomena, anorexic or bulimic phenomena, repetitive acting out or *passage à l'acte*, panic phenomena, psychosomatic phenomena, and also elementary phenomena). As described by its Greek etymology, the phenomenon is what appears, what can be seen and denotes what is given, what is shown. With the particularities of the subjectivity of the time, it's these phenomena that question us analysts, and they invite us to not retreat when scientific or standardized discourses are obsolete. Did the Anna O.s, the Elisabeth Von R.s, the Katharinas of more than a century ago not pierce, with what their symptoms shouted, the knowledge of that time?

I will quote a fragment from a 1974 conference in which Lacan said:

> Should psychoanalysis succeed, it would die out, in being but a forgotten symptom. This should not surprise it; it is the destiny of truth, as it itself established from the start—truth gets forgotten. Thus, everything depends on whether the real insists. For this to happen it is necessary that psychoanalysis should fail. One must recognize that in this respect it is right on course, and so still has a good chance of remaining a symptom. (Lacan 2019, 92)

Abiding by the title of the Conference—"Limits of Treatments, Limitations of Therapists"—it may be worth remembering that it's the analyst through their desire—the desire of the analyst—from where they preside as an agent to foster, through what's literal of the letter, a knowledge about the limit that, instead of being limiting, is the passport where the subject's course is registered.

DEPRESSION

Saturn and Melancholy, Raymond Klibansky, Erwin Panofsky, and Fritz Saxl's landmark iconological study of melancholy, states:

> The melancholic and no other represented Kant's notion of virtue. . . . The melancholic became in this way the possessor of an ideal of freedom, and the chains with which the sick melancholic used to be bound became the symbol of all the chains which free men abhor, no matter whether they shackle the slave, or decorate the courtier. The "sadness without cause" was based on his possession of a moral scale which destroyed personal happiness by the merciless revelation of his own and others' worthlessness. (Klibansky, Panofsky, & Saxl 1979, 122)

Frequently, in daily clinical practice, the consultations revolve around a state of depression that also involves feeling sad, generalized inhibition, abulia, lack of energy, and eating and sleeping disorders that vary from a pronounced decrease to rampant excess.[9]

Even though it's true that since Freud presented the particularities of mourning and melancholia in the famous 1915 text, we have used these diagnostic categories for our practice, we should reflect on what place to grant a term as widespread as that of "depression."

What differences do these terms entail: depression, mourning, and melancholia? A question that I think would allow us to move forward is whether the generalized inhibition, the difficulty in getting up that patients with depression are charged with, asthenia, and abulia are always the result of an affective loss, or could they be responses to other factors that affect the structure. I think that although phenomenologically they do not present notorious distinctions, being able to distinguish them has consequences for the direction of the treatment.

Let's start with the term "depression" as defined in the dictionary. Depression: sinking. Loss of strength. Melancholy state that makes you lose motivation. "Economic depression" is applied to the circumstantial state of an issue that suffers a decrease in activity.

From this definition, it's interesting to underline that, in addition to equating depression with melancholy, it mentions the compromise of the loss of strength, and it highlights the term's use to indicate how the market economy works.

Although they are not homogeneous terms, we can risk proposing that with mourning, melancholy, and depression the economic factor of the libidinal economy is down.

Depression is a term that has intensive and sometimes abusive use, and it currently takes up some pages in the DSM IV Manual, which has strongly propagated its use.

In DSM IV, depression is among mood disorders that include an alteration of humor (sadness). In addition, among the characteristics that said episode includes, there is a decrease in interest and capacity for pleasure in all or almost all activities, irregularities in sleep and appetite, feeling of excessive guilt, lack of energy, psychomotor retardation, and difficulty thinking, concentrating, or making decisions.

Said depressive disorder receives in this nosographic manual a classification and numbering according to the intensity of the depressive episode (mild, moderate, or severe), or according to whether it's accompanied by other peculiarities, such as psychotic phenomena or manic or hypomanic episodes (the last two are called bipolar).

Undoubtedly, like other classifications of this nature, they are meticulously descriptive in the pursuit of including the greatest number of clinical cases possible without leaving any out, avoiding the case-by-case uniqueness.

Let's go back to the question at the beginning. What place should be assigned to depression with respect to mourning and melancholia? We can affirm that the three share the phenomenological description; however, I want to propose that they are not homogeneous terms. I'll point out some questions which will allow us to delve into their distinctions.

Let's do a historical review of the term "depression" in Freudian records. We find that there is frequent use of the term "depression" in many of the clinical cases describing neuroses. Emma, Lucy, Elisabeth von R., Dora, Little Hans, Wolf man, they all suffered from depressive states.

Freud, in his *Studies on Hysteria*, proclaimed that rarely, in neurosis, there are not traits of depression and distressing expectation.

Depression seems to be one of the common denominators of what the sufferers of neurosis have. In addition to hysterical, obsessive, or phobic symptoms, the characteristics of depression seem to be present in many of those who went to the Viennese teacher to mitigate their ailments.

Nonetheless, Freud never set it apart or described it as a nosological entity in itself, he sets it aside to bring together the phenomenal characteristics of depression with mourning and melancholia, carving out their differences.

These terms are often used interchangeably and with overlap. A note by James Strachey at the beginning of the famous *Mourning and Melancholia* explains that what Freud called melancholia is what is now usually described as states of depression. This statement confirms the assessment that the father of psychoanalysis made in *Inhibition, Symptom and Anxiety*. There, speaking of that state of generalized inhibition that accompanies depressive states, he brought up the example of a patient with obsessional neurosis who was overcome by a paralyzing fatigue, for one or several days, when an occasion arose that should have thrown him into a rage. He adds, "We have here a point from which it should be possible to reach an understanding of the condition of general inhibition which characterizes states of depression, including the gravest form of them, melancholia" (Freud 1959a, 90).

Mourning, on the other hand, is the reaction to a loss, which may be more or less recent, but which, by involving some of the ideal objects, while they're objects of the subject's love, is irreplaceable and demands elaboration. It calls for the entire symbolic universe to contribute letters to correct the loss that has occurred. In that sense, no matter how painful a bereavement may be, it can be the occasion for reregistering the lack that engenders the subject, repositioning it with respect to the loss of the object, stirring it from a place of enjoyment. It is along this path that we understand why Lacan assigns a function to mourning. Recall that, if Freud proposed an elaboration for mourning, Lacan also assigned a role.

We could hazard, by way of conjecture, that in melancholia, in the instituting moments, the phallic investment didn't give birth to the object. In this time it's the gaze of the Other that sustains the anticipatory jubilation of the harmony of the mirror image, constitutive of the Ideal Ego. Nevertheless, due to avatars, the object leaves the circuit of desire; it disappears from the field of gaze.[10]

In melancholia the intense reduction in the esteem of the ego includes the loss of an object that was not in the field of consciousness, not a loss in the ego, but at the level of the "ideal ego," which in the Optical schema is presented as i(*a*). Therefore, in melancholia, the failure of the structure has repercussions at the level of the imaginary constitution of the ego.

Whereas with mourning the subject knows what they lost, with melancholia it can hardly be established which loss is being dealt with, or as Freud says, "He knows *whom* he has lost but not *what* he lost in him" (Freud 1957a, 245). This ambiguity likely has to do with an absence of libidinal investment in a mythical time of imaginary crystallization, with which melancholia puts on that durable nature that makes it so reluctant to move forward in the logical times of elaboration typical of mourning.

The melancholized body seems overwhelmed, with a heavy heart because of the weight of the object's shadow. We know the effectiveness of the imaginary over the real, and for years I have been surprised at times by the striking, dark hollowed-eyes of some of the patients who arrived with that grueling diagnosis.

With melancholia—it seems appropriate to reserve the term melancholia for some very severe cases of subjective collapse—sometimes the demand is for a drug, "give me something." I think I read there a grievance for something to intercede in the real through the incorporation of a body, of a substantial object, the drug. Will this demand represent the intake of the totemic meal, the possibility of incorporating a father, a piece of the father's body?

Addressing these issues, I found in the Seminar X, *Anxiety* (1962–1963) that Lacan mentioned two cycles of the subject's positioning in its constitution with respect to the Other and the loss of an object that this operation involves.

He called the first cycle "mourning-desire" and the other one "mania-melancholia." The first conveys that the subject, faced with the real of life, has a disposition to process losses, and the function of mourning rehabilitates the path of desire. The mania-melancholy cycle, however, wouldn't allow the auspiciousness of the work of mourning. Taking that phrase from the Seminar XI, *The Four Fundamental Concepts of Psychoanalysis* (1964) that states that "a lack engendered from the previous time that serves to reply to the lack raised by the following time" (Lacan 1978, 215). We could say that in this cycle, there's no inscription of that original, preceding lack to then respond to the deficiencies that are subsequently brought forth.

Lacan explicitly stated that in the mania-melancholia cycle, what is at stake is the non-function of *a*. What does it mean that there is no function of *a* in the structure? We know of the constitution of *a* by its function in the phantom. What consequences does the omission of its function have? If there is no function of *a*, is it possible for there to be a function of mourning?

I would dare to say that, if there is no function of *a*, then it'd be very unlikely that a subject immersed in melancholy or mania have a predisposition to the establishment of analytical transference. On occasion, it's common to hear an absence of credibility in their speech, an extreme negativism, accompanied by a sharp decrease in energy, disinterest, and apathy.

Melancholia appertains to an impossible mourning due to the absence of the function of the object *a*. Maneuvers in the transference, from the records of the imaginary and the real, will realize the vouch for the possibility of the analyst lodging as a countenance of the object *a* so that the analysis can run its course. The *aprés-coup* will speak of its effectiveness.

An event from an everyday chronicle (I say it like that because of the frequency with which it's occurring lately) led me to a hypothesis that I'll lay out here.

A patient entered a session and told me that a couple of days ago he had been robbed. He relates how he had withdrawn money from the bank to make a payment on an apartment, and he took a taxi which stopped halfway there. Two armed men came up, in a state of exhilaration. Aiming a revolver at him, and abusing him, they took the money he was carrying, and then threw him out of the taxi on an unknown street.

He explained, referring to the sad episode, "They leave you shaking, they yell at you, they insult you, they make you panic. You feel impotent and irate."

What he said was that he hadn't been able to recover his energies, that he felt weak. He explained that in itself the theft of the money had brought him complications, but there was something that affected him more than the money they had stolen. He felt strengthless, exhausted. This state lasted for a few weeks. Later he brought up some dreams, one of a boy imprisoned in a well, who was making a great effort to get out, but was unsuccessful. He associated it with the confinement with his mother, and her mistreatment of him when he wanted to go out. Then, that generalized inhibition gave way.

However, for a long time he still referred to the assault as a situation of intimidation in front of a crazy and armed Other, who could abuse his defenselessness and end his life.

As I was saying, I tried to distinguish between depression, melancholia, and mourning to consider what should be the direction of the treatment. My question was regarding the overwhelmed, disinterested, fatigued, weak, lethargic state which persists or recurs in some cases of depression or latent melancholia, in which the loss of a loved object is not clearly distinguished; it's not cut out in their speech, but what prevails, more so than their sad mood, is reluctance, lack of energy, and sometimes fatigue. I ask: Do these clinical manifestations that beset some patients with neurotic depressions or melancholias be related to a positioning before an Other, to the arbitrariness of an Other that in one way or another is lethal, deadly for subjectivation?

The story of this young man brought me back to the description that Lacan offers in Seminar X, of anxiety before the praying mantis, a homicidal insect, a paradigm of a threatening Other, under which the fate of a subject hangs on in extreme defenselessness.

What do we mean when we say that the Other can be deadly to the subject in different ways? The hypothesis that I propose is that, from each of the registers, the Other can be lethal to the access to subjectivity of the human offspring.

The Other, as Lacan repeatedly says, is the place where the signifying chain that governs everything that can be made present in the subject is situated. That Other is essentially, genuinely required for subjectivity. The problematic thing about this is that on the one hand, that Other is essential for subjectivity, but, in addition, it's an Other in which, essentially, the drive is what becomes manifest, and the drive is always the death drive.

So, a first hypothesis that I would like to propose is that, while with mourning it's all about the reaction because of the conscious loss of a loved object, with depression and melancholia, the loss remains subtracted from consciousness. Therefore, in these two clinical presentations, the direction of the treatment requires prioritizing the passage through the framework of the subject's relationship with the Other, and to break down what the Other could not yield, forfeiting for the libidinal gain of the human offspring.

In the third conference, Lacan presents a Borromean knot where he places *life* in the register of the real, *body* in that of the imaginary, and *death* in that of the symbolic.

Continuing our train of thought, and playing with these terms—*life*, *body*, and *death*—we can wager that if the lethal aspect of the Other is in the register of the real, the hegemonic register of life, it's the life of the *infans* that will be at serious risk due to the shortcoming in lavish care. The Other did not offer their life, their real time for such nursing, which are essential for parenting.

When lethality covers the imaginary field, it's in the *body*, in the image of the body (Lacan writes "body" in the ring of the imaginary), instead of the agalmatic shine that the gaze gives off when it comes from love, the shadow falls. There's no agalmatic investment of the ego. There's no joy in front of the mirror because of the harmony of the reflected body. Melancholia, then, ensues.

Silvia Amigo in her book *Clínica de los fracasosdelfantasma* (1999) defines melancholia as a pathology within the imaginary field of narcissism. She proposes that in the Borromean knot, the paradigm of the subjective structure lacks the tracing of the imaginary border of the object *a*, that pierces the imaginary, which creates the $(-\varphi)$. The $(-\varphi)$ is the libidinal operative reserve which a subject relies on to interact with their peers. It's the libido available for investing the objects of the world. It's created by the gaze's circuit of the drive in the mirror stage.

In contrast, with latent melancholia or depression, which permanently relapse and find overwhelming difficulties in entering the pathways of desire, what I propose is thinking of desire as being drugged. The Other, who is primordial on these occasions, it seems to me, is hoisted to a place of fullness, skimping on offering their death. If the Other admits they are a mortal being, they offer their death, offer their castration, and encourage the subject to find the unique lanes of desire, the strokes with which to identify themselves beyond the Other, beyond the ideal ego that the Other proposed.

We believe that in this aspect to differentiate mourning from depression, we find the developments of Ricardo Díaz Romero where he proposes that while with mourning it's about "the loss of an object of love," depression would be a reaction relative to the phallic value and castration.[11]

That the Other offer their death implies knowing that they're mortal, withstanding that at the level of the son, of the offspring, they do not possess a comprehensive or preconceived knowledge, and admitting that they don't possess a totalizing knowledge of the future. Then, they will be able to withstand the hesitations and tolerate the anguish of the times of growth and impasses that cause the inexorable encounters with the real in the constitution of the structure.

OFFERING DEATH

On occasion, we detect that those who suffer are imprisoned, trapped in a position that condemns them to be absolutely contingent on finding answers in a knowledge constructed deductively, which stems from another (while being similar) to which they assign the dimension of absolute Other (capitalized and without a bar). They seem to be halted in an eternally infantile position, in which they risk no act that involves their responsibility as a subject. They tend to prefer shying away from their desire, which keeps them in a persistent lethargic and depressive state. If the instituting Other has offered their body while in real time, and their body as an imaginary support of love to care for and rear these subjects, what clinical speech practice detects is that what the Other didn't yield was their death. It's a death that governs the symbolic dimension to propitiate the emergence of a desiring subject that definitively abandons the obsequious place of a puppet.

The following clinical case eloquently illustrated this.

Patricia first came in for consultation eight years ago when she was twenty-four years old. She had just graduated with a BA in Literature, after which she fell into a deep depression. When we met, her worried parents had taken her to different professionals that tried to prescribe her different kinds of antidepressants, without any of them bettering her condition.

In the first interview, she told me that after she graduated, she fell into a pit. She didn't understand what had happened, but she didn't want to go out, nothing interested her. She wanted to stay in bed all the time. She didn't have any strength. With a hint of a smile, she said, "They didn't expect me, I came as a little gift." Due to the career her father had chosen during her infancy and adolescence, they repeatedly had to move all over the country. At the last location where they moved to before settling down in Buenos Aires, she had begun studying at a university. In spite of being very thrilled, she had to drop out because of the family's next relocation to the capital city. That stage of her university life had stayed with her as a time of much happiness.

Her mother was the one that registered her to study Literature here at a private university, a degree that had nothing to do with what she had previously chosen to study. When I asked her about this, she said, justifying her mother, that her mother liked to read a lot, and that she also liked literature. She wrote poems. Thus, she studied obediently until she graduated.

She related that directly after graduating they offered her a job as a substitute at a school, and that faced with the indifference and reluctance that plagued her, she would only get up to go to work. Her "dad was the one that wrote the lessons."

Patricia described several situations of her life where, because of not knowing "what was right and what was wrong," she'd let others, usually her parents, decide things for her. She repeatedly related that her mother, faced with her daughter's complaints about not being able to complete her studies at the other university, said to her that if she had put up more of a fight, like her siblings, they would've let her stay there.

Time and time again, Patricia recalled how, being the youngest of her siblings, she had become fixed as a little girl. That's how they always treated her, as the whimsical, unhappy one. They didn't take her requests seriously.

The relationships that Patricia laid out had the characteristic of consisting of a phase of fleeting idealization that rapidly flowed out in a deep disillusionment and the consequent dissolution of the relationship. The longest lasting relationship was with a young addict, who she maintained a tormented relationship with that was difficult to end.

In the beginning, whenever the memory of an incident where her mother clearly appeared to devalue or degrade her reared its head, Patricia would try to justify her actions in a thousand ways, as if trying to protect her. She appeared to be on an untouchable pedestal. She knew what was best for Patricia.

She told of how her father, a lieutenant in the armed forces, had to leave the country when she was born because he had participated in a failed military coup, which resulted in him being exiled for a year. She related that he had always been very affectionate with her. She has a recurring dream where she feels like she's breathing with the same nose as her father. She would wake up startled and anguished.

Frequently, she would enter the session complaining about the amount of class hours that she had to accrue at different schools in order to have a decent salary. She said that she liked giving classes, teaching, being with the students, but she didn't have time for other things. She was thinking that she'd like to take a trip, sign up for a writing workshop, or do something different. Nonetheless, the weekends were always the same, staying in bed all day. There she felt shielded.

In a second moment, she began to ask herself if she'd always be like that. Something needed to change. She decided to take a weekend trip to that city where she had started studying at the university, where she had left friends, and where the decisive, creative Patricia that she longed for had stayed. She returned from that experience very encouraged. She began fantasizing about living there. However, after repeated trips, she admitted that nothing was like how she left it during her adolescence.

One time while on vacation, after putting it off repeatedly, she arranged a trip to New York, where one of her friends lived. She returned from the trip delighted, even though she said that she'd like to organize another trip to visit places, not to go visit someone.

During this period she also began to speak of her desire to move. She complained that the apartment she had lived in was picked by her mother, and that she would've liked to live in another type of apartment, a recycled antique style. When she told her mother, she quickly tried to derail her moving plan in different ways.

On that occasion she came in for consultation indignant and said, "My mom is a steamroller. She runs me over. She's like a train. She sweeps me away."

That's how Patricia was able to make the determination to move to a house that she picked. She had placed far too many expectations on this move. As could be supposed, soon after this change materialized, she remarked that this wasn't the change she pretended. It needed to come from a different direction, that she changed locations, but things definitely didn't change.

She started to talk about her poems during the sessions. This coincided with an author's invitation to her book presentation, with which the outline of a space for her, that wasn't in that other idealized city nor inside the walls of a new apartment, began to come into view.

If depression describes a mood that is present in both mourning and melancholia, it seemed to me that there were differences that could provide interesting elements for thinking about the direction of treatments.

With mourning, treatment generally goes through the times of elaboration that consists of the piece-by-piece detachment of the libido, such that the libido returns to the ego and the lack of the subject, a way of taking up again the paths of desire.

With melancholia, the lost object that causes depression can hardly be identified. As Patricia repeated, the issue was finding a place, a place in the Other, which we could maybe say houses instead of runs the subject over, mortifying the desire.

The lethality of the Other operates in the symbolic register. The names assigned to the subject withhold them and make them permanently stumble, without finding the propitiatory places to make their dormant desires fruitful.

NOTES

1. We use the term "act" as Lacan used it in his unpublished Seminar XV, *The Psychoanalytic Act* (1967–1968). There, some of the premises of the act are: it is significant, determines a beginning, has to do with the desire and commitment of the subject, breaks the repetition compulsion and inaugurates a new desire.
2. See the chapter titled "The Issue of Mourning and the Status of the Object."
3. This is referencing the suicide of the businessman Alfredo Yabrán, who was accused of killing the journalist José Luis Cabezas, and which stirred up the public opinion.
4. See Vegh, I. 1991. *El melancólicoobjetodelmaldecir* [The Melancholy Object of the Curse] in *Matices* [Nuances]. Buenos Aires: Agalma.
5. For more information on this topic, see Aries, P. 2008. *The Hour of Our Death*. New York: Random House.
6. Translated by Gabriel Sarmiento.
7. Work presented at the "Annual Conference of the General Belgrano Hospital," Buenos Aires, 1998.
8. Translator's note: the Spanish word *borde*, used here, which best translates as edge, has been rendered border to maintain the relation between border and borderline, whereas the Spanish word *frontera*, which best translates as border, is rendered frontier.
9. This work was accomplished as a product of the Questions Cartel of the Clinic and Subjectivity of the Era. Members: Miriam Bercovich, M. Cristina delVillar, Graciela Jasiner, and Liliana Lamovsky.
10. A more detailed look at this topic is given in Part 2, "The Issue of Mourning and the Status of the Object."
11. SeeDíaz Romero, R. 1999. *La pregunta por la técnica del psicoanálisis* (The Question about the Technique of Psychoanalysis). Rosario: Homo Sapiens.

BIBLIOGRAPHY

Arendt, H. 1968. "Walter Benjamin: 1892–40" in *Men in Dark Times*. New York: Harcourt, 153–206.

Aries, P. 2008. *The Hour of Our Death*. New York: Random House.

Díaz Romero, R. 1999. *La pregunta por la técnica del psicoanálisis* [The Question about the Technique of Psychoanalysis]. Rosario: Homo Sapiens.

Freud, S. 1959a. "Inhibitions, Symptoms, and Anguish" in *SE, Vol. XX*, 77–177.

Klibansky, R., Panofsky, E., & Saxl, F. 1979.*Saturn and Melancholy¸Liechtenstein: Kraus Reprint.*

Lacan, J. 1971–1972. *The Seminar of Jacques Lacan: The Knowledge of the Psychoanalyst, 1971–1972.* Unpublished translation by Cormac Gallagher.

Lacan, J. 1978. *The Seminar of Jacques Lacan: The Four Fundamental Concepts of Psychoanalysis: Book XI*. New York: W.W. Norton & Company.

Lacan, J. 2014. *Anxiety: the Seminar of Jacques Lacan, Book X*. Cambridge: Polity.

Lacan, J. 2019. "The Third," *The Lacanian Review, Get Real*, Issue 07, Spring, 83–112.

Vegh, I. 1991. *El melancólicoobjetodelmaldecir* [The Melancholy Object of the Curse] in *Matices* [Nuances]. Buenos Aires: Agalma.

Chapter 7

Mourning in the *Polis*

THE FUNERAL RITE: CONSEQUENCES AND THE AFTERMATH OF ITS IMPEDIMENTS

> The works that, in the proverbial significance of their meaning, support the guiding, paradigmatic value of specific unanswered questions whose treatment, far from weakening us, strengthens us are classics. If we continue reading Sophocles, it is not, first and foremost, to know, generation after generation, the past, but to once again draw near to the enigma that hints at the fact of living. It is the amazing fact of being present that finds an echo in the roots of our elders.
>
> —Santiago Kovadloff (1996)

There are two classical works, *Hamlet* and *Antigone*, which Lacan deals with, in consecutive Seminars VI and VII, *Desire and Its Interpretation* (1958–1959) and *The Ethics of Psychoanalysis* (1959–1960), respectively, to address the consequences that subject subjectivity to its impediment, the cancellation of the times of pain. In both, the tragic end of the life of the young protagonists, Prince Hamlet and Antigone, is closely linked to the sparing of the funeral rites and honor worthy and proper of humans.

Let us start with the Shakespearean drama. There, Lacan emphatically places the importance attached to the funeral rituals agreed upon by society, in order to deal with and tolerate that hole in reality that the death of a loved one causes. In the first place, the ceremonies and community rites that accompany mourning bring satisfaction because of the insufficient elements of the significant order. He asks:

> What, in the final analysis, are funeral rites designed to do? To propitiate [*satisfaire à*] what we call the memory of the departed. And what do these rites involve if not the total, massive intervention, from hell to heaven, of the entire symbolic system [*jeusymbolique*] (Lacan 2019, 337).

Furthermore, he adds, "There is nothing that can fill the hole in the real with signifiers unless it is the totality of the signifier itself" (Lacan 2019, 337). How should we understand this significant totality if it is not in a dimension of the symbolic that exceeds the subject, which concerns the entire community? In this line, the character of the funeral rites is described as macrocosmic:

> The work of mourning is carried out at the level of logos—I am saying this so as not to say at the level of the group or community, even though the group and the community as culturally organized naturally support this. (Lacan 2019, 337)

When this is not accomplished in this way, it's not uncommon for the dead not to die, and their wraiths continue to visit the living in hallucinogenic appearances. This is how Lacan labels the emergence of the ghost of the father before Hamlet's astonished gaze. When the work of mourning is impeded, the phenomena in which the mourning is revealed frequently to be related to psychosis. Hallucinations, *passage à l'acte*, permanent actings, and so on begin to manifest instead of what concerns a work of elaboration, memories, dreams, failures, linked with the absent person. The latter denotes a considerable effort of attachment undertaken by the psychic apparatus that translates into the manifestation of a set of formations of the unconscious through which a significant recomposition is operated, effective for repositioning the subject.

The spectral appearances as a phenomenon correspond to a hallucinatory image, the result of the annulment, distortion, or reduction of the funeral rites. Different peoples have given them various names generally associated with local religious beliefs; thus, in the interior of our country, figures of this nature are embodied in "the bad light" and "the soul in sorrow." The need to assign a name to what inexorably lacks representation seems to dominate these beliefs, along with the idea that only through popular myth and magical thinking can an identity be granted.

Prince Hamlet's father is killed by his brother Claudius, who immediately afterward marries his sister-in-law and usurps the kingdom. Hamlet ironically points out that the funeral of the dead king barely receives minimal funeral honors with these verses: "The funeral baked meats did coldly furnish forth the marriage tables."

As a son, Hamlet will be affected in a pathetic and multifaceted way by that homicide of his father and his meager funeral. As the father's specter confesses to him, he had been surprised by death "in the blossom of his sins." Whereupon his soul would not receive the posthumous blessing. This betrays the father's image, whose version is more on the side of the sinful than that of the one who imparts the law governing the symbolic order. The place of honor of the father falls apart throughout the series of events that happen to him, being reduced to a ghostly specter that uses his son to demand that he avenge him and settle his accounts with those who betrayed him.

Difficult crossroads from which the young Hamlet is left without escape, lost in his desires, begin to carry out a continuum of unchosen actions—actings—that separate him from the course of his desires. He condemns and abandons the beloved woman, Ophelia. He embarks on a journey with two rascals who were carrying his death sentence. He kills Polonius by mistake. A set of troubles and setbacks keep happening until they lead to the final fall, his own death, at the same time that he fulfills the task that his father commissioned, that is, to kill Claudius.

It was the irony of fate that made it that upon recovering the usurped place that corresponded to Hamlet, which inaugurated him as king, heir to the throne, would simultaneously result in the deadly dagger from his opponent instantly bringing his death.

In the classes of the Seminar VII, *The Ethics of Psychoanalysis* (1959–1960) in which Lacan is dedicated to commenting on the tragedy of *Antigone*, the emphasis also lies on the value it had for the protagonist to honor the remains of his brother. Her desire leads her to carry out, transgressing Creon's arbitrary order, Polynices's funeral.

In the case of *Antigone*, there is also a structural crack in the paternal function. The incestuous union of Oedipus and Yocasta having begotten Antigone, Ismene, Polynices, and Eteocles, throughout the tragedy the consequences of such a heritage weights on the life of the protagonists. This is stated by the young woman at the beginning of the play: "Ismene, my sister, true child of my own mother, do you know any evil out of all the evils bequeathed by Oedipus that Zeus will not fulfill for the two of us in our lifetime?" (Sophocles 2003, 53)

Creon had forbidden the funeral of Polynices. He had left the corpse rotting, abandoned at the gates of the city, reduced to carrion, soon to be eaten by birds of prey. Antigone will oppose this order by disobeying it, rebelling, and burying it as dictated by divine law. Lacan, in the class of June 6, 1960, reflects on the logic that urges Antigone in these terms:

> One cannot finish off someone who is a man as if he were a dog. One cannot be finished with his remains simply by forgetting that the register of being of someone who was identified by a name has to be preserved by funeral rites. (Lacan 1997, 279)

The imperativeness with which Antigone wants to bury her brother throughout the tragedy responds to what we call "subjective function of mourning." It refers to the ethical value that concerns the survivor who does not give in to any impediment in undertaking the funeral rituals, and then the commemoration for the dignity of the loved one. Burying the corpse, honoring the remains of the dead, placing an epitaph are symbolic marks, traces of civility. When that treatment for the dead is truncated or prevented, ignoring the "unwritten but unmovable laws," as Sophocles' heroine reminds him, is a sign of a severe collapse and breakdown of the ethical values of society.

Antigone's discourse shows in an exemplary way the characteristic of being a unique object that a loved one has for the one who survives him, independent of any value or moral judgment that can be made about his person. In the case of this tragedy, the characteristic of uniqueness is caved in, as eloquently expressed by the young woman, that since her father and mother died, no longer can she have another brother. She has lost something that is irreplaceable, and to register her passage through the land, it's absolutely essential to follow the steps that the ritual of mourning demands. Burying him is a way of naming him, reassigning him the human identity that every mortal deserves. It's what allows the loss to be registered as missing.

What in other chapters we call "subjective function of mourning" refers to the ethical value that concerns the subject who doesn't cease to carry out the rituals and the commemoration of the loved one to confer the dignity that the defunct deserves.

Lacan expresses this when he attributes to the operation of the rite the attempt to match up the breach opened by the mourning—that which he had called the hole in the real—with the greater breach, the point *x*, the symbolic absence. Just like when he worked Hamlet's drama in reference to mourning, Lacan emphasizes that, although pain is preserved for the private and family environment, there is a portion of mourning that needs to be processed in the public and social spheres. He suggests the hypothesis that the outcome of this story could have been different if the community had wanted to forgive Polynices for the betrayal of his people and perform the same funeral honors they performed for Eteocles.

Would it be abusive to think that the high price that Antigone pays to sustain the ethical commitment of burying the remains of Polynices and surrendering her life to that cause divulges her relationship with desire in its *purest form*? (emphasis ours) (Lacan 1997, 282). This is how Lacan defines it in the class of June 6, 1960, when he calls it "the desire of the mother" (Lacan 1997, 283). It seems to imply that it is a virgin desire, which has not been impregnated by the paternal metaphor, hence the deadly consequences.[1]

Louis-Vincent Thomas, in his book *Anthropologie de la mort* (1975), proposes that the attitude toward death—and the corpse—would be the essential feature through which man partially escapes nature and becomes a cultured animal. He comments that among living animal species, humans are the only one for whom death is omnipresent in the course of life (even if it isn't in fantasy), the only one that surrounds death with a complex funeral ritual and loaded with symbolism. Humans are the only one for which biological death is constantly overtaken by death as a cultural fact.

The analysis of the mortuary rituals carried out by the Bantu tribe is interesting, as described by E. Ortigues, as it reflects how the death of one member affects the entire group, and, therefore, it's necessary to enter and process the mourning as a group. I'll detail it below. Death poses a problem given that it has just inflicted a loss on them. It introduces a negative sign. The community, through rituals, will try to reverse it into a positive sign, as an increase in life. Since within the system all terms are community based, that which affects one has an impact on all others. Thus, the first moment is characterized by the entry into mourning, which consists in extending the negative sign through prohibitions that apply to all domains of collective life: food, breeding, agriculture, livestock raising, and even the use of names linked to the person of the deceased. These actions indicate an intense shared sensitivity, agreed upon by the loss. In the second instance, the movement is reversed. Appealing to what linguists call zero-grade metaphor, the domestic fire is replaced by ritual fire, which will precede the reversal of prohibitions and initiate the series of substitutions. For example, when it comes to food, white products (milk, flour, beans) are adopted and lustral water is used to clean the house. Therefore, this stage of exiting the mourning is also called "bleaching" the mourning. In summary, the negative value that the loss denotes in the real world becomes the revitalization of community values, dietary plans, sexual life, agriculture, and so on in the symbolic plane.

Burial ceremonies, shared by the tribal family as a whole, guarantee their immutability. That is, the individual dies but the family doesn't die. Through this ritual performed together, the family identifies itself with life. As a community that shares in the rituals of mourning, it affirms its perpetuation in the continuation of the generations.

As Patrick Guyomard states in *La jouissance du tragique* (1992), funerals separate the living from the dead and allow the living to live without being obsessed with their ghosts.

From the primitive tribes, to Greco-Roman antiquity, to medieval and modern times, mourning has been more social than individual. According to Philippe Aries, it's from the twentieth century onward that a new landscape appears in the most individualized and bourgeois parts of the West, which is the progressive suppression of mourning. He says that in the history of civilization, it's the first time that such a rejection manifests itself so openly. The historian, in the exegesis he does on the subject of his book, The *Hour of Our*

Death (1982), he emphasizes that it was at the same time that this attitude toward death emerged that psychoanalysis knew to warn, through the pen of its creator, of the extreme risk and danger of such a rejection.[2]

These comments allude to a push to avoid death that was adapted in the early twentieth century in Western societies, gradually rebuffing and relegating any manifestation or expression of funerary sentimentality with greater intensity.

With regard to this issue, we can't fail to mention that genocidal massacres where the victims were stripped of their human identity and had their bodies condemned to unlimited horrors and humiliations also grew out of this century.

This is the case of the atrocities committed under the Nazi regime, with its concentration camps and its gas chambers, or the state terrorism that installed itself in Argentina between 1976 and 1983. Here too we were struck with extermination, human denigration, deaths and births without documentation or with falsified registrations.

The term "disappeared" with which the military dictatorship baptized its victims is quite fitting in articulating the criminal endeavor to reduce people and their remains to bodies without identities, without names. State terrorism, to try to ensure impunity, implemented the designation of the "disappeared" to brand those who were kidnapped, tortured and killed. The forced disappearance of a person has a deeply sinister dimension due to the turmoil generated in those close to them, the pain infinitely multiplied by the legal defenselessness that stains each family drama and by the abolition of the right to mourn that makes it impossible to begin the process that partially reduces the pain.

In both cases, the general public's silence prevailed, which was perhaps what allowed these massacres to reach such magnitude. Silence that, though fueled by terror, doesn't cease to convey a certain implicit and involuntary complicity.

Due to the circumstances described, that which demands social and public participation in mourning and that compromises the course of the historical and political life of the peoples, was seriously affected. That is why the historical reconstruction of memory becomes so essential. Paul Ricoeur[3] brings an interesting nuance to help think about the multifaceted mourning caused by those abject infamies of humanity and says:

> "It's necessary to be able to face the unforgivable. Why? Forgiveness is difficult because it hinges on a double enterprise: the work memory and the work of mourning. . . . And mourning isn't limited to grieving for those we've lost. We must also think about mourning for an explanation. (Bermond, 1998)

There is hardly an explanation for the atrocities which human cruelty can commit. Every paragraph of the history of mankind is afflicted by some disgrace of such nature. Should there also be mourning in order to comprehend? However, and with a glimmer of optimism, we can affirm that the legal actions of the Spanish judge BaltazarGarzón, referring to non-"immunity" for those who commit crimes against humanity, indicates an advance for civilization against barbarism.

It should be remembered that, in civilization, a body, from birth to death, receives identifying, symbolic marks that grant it human dignity, ratifying its genealogy and registering it within the culture, assigning it a name.

It is the State that extends a birth or death certificate that materializes into an identification certificate. Due to the type of relationship with the loved object, a topic that we developed in the preceding chapters, it wouldn't seem inappropriate to conjecture that, once its loss has taken place, for any work of mourning to begin, it's essential that the loss is recognized by a third party. Hence, in our civilization, it's customary for someone else to give out the so-called death certificate to the bereaved.

In the face of the excesses committed during these human massacres, this fact of the omission of supplying death certificates probably seems like a tiny matter. Nevertheless, we believe that it continues to be relevant as far as considering the viable conditions necessary for mourning to commence.

Psychoanalysis argues that there is no registration in the unconscious of one's own death. In fact, Freud came to say, verbatim, that in the unconscious we're all convinced of our immortality. That's why what becomes intolerable is the death of another, of our peer in whom the various modes of our love are bound together. It's intolerable because the other loved one becomes a narcissistic point for the subject, where "you" and "me" become indistinguishable. Jean Allouch proposes that whoever is mourning enacts their loss by supplementing it with what he calls a "small piece of themselves," which becomes the object of that grieving sacrifice. That little piece is neither yours nor mine. It is of itself, and therefore, of you and me, but only as long as you and I remain indistinguishable.

That is the reason why we consider that the acknowledgment and certification of an Other is essential. It represents the social body and, in the symbolic act of issuing a death certificate, enables the possibility of letting the work of mourning begin. The omission of this act fosters the redoubling of that first period of mourning that is characterized by denial, not wanting to have anything to do with it. In that case the slogan that identifies the "Mothers of the Plaza de Mayo"—"Appearance with Life"—ceases to seem like a naïve claim, but is instead fully substantiated. From the moment nobody told them that their children had died, this slogan came trying to avoid the reduplication or even the multiplication of the disavowing nature that permeated those dark pages of history. We'll continue our reflection with what Fernando Ulloa said in the Seminar on Critical Analysis of Argentine Reality, published on *Página/12* on February 4, 2000. He says,

> Appearance with life . . . one wonders, What do you mean appearance with life? Of course the phrase finished very boldly, and this is implicit in the intention of the slogan. It's to have their loved ones show up alive, or being told who killed them, who is to blame, and that justice be done. The modern utopia thus defined is a critical utopia, an advocate of critical thinking.

Through the death certificate, it's verified at the public level that a loss has occurred that affects the whole. Certificates—of death or of birth—have the function of legitimizing the civilizing social bond between a subject and the community to which they belong.

The concealment of the lists that had the names of the "disappeared" plunges the entire community into an impasse of reduplication of denial that prevents initiating the elaboration of mourning, and instead creates serious tears in the social fabric. These phenomena are consequences and the aftermath of that crushing of subjectivity, of the abolition of transcendental marks that distinguish a subject

Three circumstances, among others, implanted in the perverted social scene, violate and hinder the possibility of beginning the mourning process that relieves the pain of loss. Firstly, the kidnapping method used, the concentration camps and disappearance of the people that left their relatives in total ignorance and helplessness about the fate of those detained. Secondly, just how cruel the massacres were (gas chambers, "death flights" where they were dropped from planes, torture, mutilation). Lastly, the impunity they had with regards to the events that occurred.

Let us end with the poignant words of Hector Schmucler, father of one of the disappeared,

> each missing person is the center of a drama. When it ceases to be a numerical figure—useful for statistics, but insufficient for memory—each missing person mortifies the conscience of all men without any attenuation. When the missing person is a son, the father knows that the absence's imprint won't stop accompanying him, and yet he hopes for some rest: the moment when the disappeared person reappears as dead, that is, the moment when they recover their dignity as a human being, which the others tried to deprive them of.[4]

MOURNING: A PRIVATE OR PUBLIC RITUAL

In a book that just recently appeared in our midst, *Mothers in Mourning* (1998), its author, Nicole Loraux, mentions that in the Agora of Athens—the central square of the city, a public space dedicated to politics as understood by democracy—the Temple of the Mother of the gods can be found. This building called Metroon, where the worship of mothers took place, was also destined to keep the public archives of Athens. Thus, it's at this site, that maternal den, that protects and safeguards the laws and decrees of the Polis.

This beautiful coincidence closely links mothers with a civic function in the community, which is to become guardians of the rights, preserved in writing, of the city, to preserve the memory of the norms that legalize and regulate the relations between men.

In Ancient Greece, women lacked the rank of citizens. Their civic function was exercised through motherhood. By bringing children into the world, they created the future soldiers who would defend the Polis. Some, like the Spartans, were extremely proud to send them to the front lines.

For these Hellenic women, who were absolutely excluded from the political scene, destined almost exclusively to reproduce the paternal brand, the Greek tradition unanimously recognizes them as having served as the guardians of memory.

Memory is closely linked to the act of remembering, of elaborating the losses, of carrying out the ceremonies consecrated to the dead. This task was reserved particularly for the females of the community.

As Loraux points out, and as the Greek tragedies of *Antigone* by Sophocles and *The Suppliants* by Aeschylus perfectly exemplify, the confluence of mourning and women is not random. Fulfilling the funeral ceremonies that dignify the fallen corresponds essentially to the feminine side.

However, it seems as though, looking at severe legislation about this, that the Athenian Acropolis of the fifth-century BC feared female mourning. Thus, funerals began to be restricted by decrees to only take place in the private sphere. They resorted to submitting the laments and expressions of feminine pain to multiple restrictions, aimed at discounting the maternal suffering of the irreparable loss of a child.

Drawing nearer to our own recent history, could we find any specific foundation that made it precisely the mothers and grandmothers who registered under a new name in the social bond, at the center of the urban fabric, a name that identifies them as the Mothers of the Plaza?

It's undeniable that the female enigma has produced discoveries in each era. At the end of the nineteenth century, it was the conversational feature of the female body, its ability to symptomatize, that challenged the scientists of the time, and prompted them to create new paradigms in order to be able to think about the subject's suffering. That's how psychoanalysis was born.

We could conjecture that this encounter between the feminine and mourning isn't accidental, but that it's rooted in its fundamental lack, that is, castration.

This is not much different that it's position with respect to the "son," a privileged signifier in the series of variables of the symbolic equation. To her body, in its real, symbolic and imaginary dimensions, the willingness to have a child is immanent to then detach themselves from the child, and accompany them as they cede them to the culture.

Being a mother implies a permanent renunciation—which I see as re-enunciating the absence—of the one who was flesh of her flesh. Having nestled them in her womb, after that inaugural and poignant separation that is birth, in a second act of detachment, she'll hand them over to the social structure in which they live.

Thus, the task of motherhood entails "mourning" the different stages of growth of their children, positioning themselves in a creative and different way during each of them.

When these renunciations, symbolic mournings, are canceled by the death of a child, the monstrosity of such an irreparable loss, a hole in the real that leaves her without an identity, can drive a mother crazy. There doesn't exist a word that denotes a mother who loses a child,[5] while widows and orphans do have that appellation.

It's an unmentionable that has no reference in our natural laws. It goes against what they indicate. It's irrational, nonsense.

When that irrationality is reinforced by the epithet of missing persons, when they are fiercely thrown into the waters of anonymity, isn't this even more maddening?

Mourning is the reaction to the loss of a loved one, and in that sense it's a distinctly personal and private rite. But when in a society where there is a mandate to forget, to deny history, to pardon the crimes committed against their children, and to call them missing, mourning is stalled. Then the dead cannot die. The ghostly apparitions then wander incessantly. Portions of mourning become impossible to go through. The logical periods that mourning entails so that it doesn't become endless remain inaccessible.

Faced with this and because of this, registering a name in the social sphere—Mothers of the Plaza—reflects the only way to make a public record and make the singularity of each mourning resonate in the collective structure, which had remained silenced, numbed by fear.

In order to not lose themselves in the face of the irremediability of what was lost, meeting and marching together as the Mothers of the Plaza fulfills the subjetivizing function of creating a supplementary name where there is no possible substitution. A way to name themselves precisely to not disappear. A way to go through that mourning that, although it's probably endless, frightens once and for all the threat of repetition.

We know of the serious consequences that could lead to indifference, concealment, and impunity of traumatic events in the coming generations.

Therefore, if the disappearance of a child can drive a mother crazy, let there be no confusion. There were and still are some that did not yield. In exchange for surrendering to illness or madness, they provided a foundational act that honors our dead, but above all dignifies the future children of our society.

NOTES

1. With respect to this, on numerous occasions the attitude of the Mothers of the Plaza de Mayo has been compared to that of Sophocles' Antigone. In spite of knowing how she wanted to fight them in the beginning, and the inflicted deaths, it appears significant to us that they accomplished registering a name that identifies them in their pain, and that they procured a public space to establish the mourning in the social scene. See the article "Mourning: A Private or Public Ritual" in this same book.

2. We suppose that he's referencing Freud's 1915 article *Reflections on War and Death*

3. Bermond, D. 1998. "Entrevista a Paul Ricoeur. Afrontar lo imperdonable," *La Nación*, June 24th 1998. https://www.lanacion.com.ar/cultura/afrontar-lo-imperdonable-nid213659/

4. *Página/12*, editorial note, year 1999.

5. We mentioned previously that only in Hebrew do there exist terms—*abshakul* and *emshkula*—to denominate the condition of a mother and father, respectively, that lose a child.

BIBLIOGRAPHY

Allouch, J. 2006. *Erotique du deuilautemps de la mortsèche*. Paris: Distribution Distique Diffusion Stendhal.

Bermond, D. 1998. "Entrevista a Paul Ricoeur. Afrontar lo imperdonable," *La Nación*, June 24th 1998. https://www.lanacion.com.ar/cultura/afrontar-lo-imperdonable-nid213659/

Kovadloff, S. 1996. *Lo irremediable*. Buenos Aires: Ed. Emecé.

Lacan, J. 1997. *The Seminar of Jacques Lacan: The Ethics Of Psychoanalysis. Book VII*, New York: Norton & Co.

Lacan, J. 2019. *The Seminar of Jacques Lacan: Desire and its Interpretation. Book VI*, Cambridge: Polity

Sophocles 2003. *Antigone*. New York: Oxford University Press, trans. by Reginald Gibbons and Charles Segal.

Ulloa, F. 2000. "Sociedad y crueldad," *Página/12*, January 4, 2000.

Bibliography

Abraham, K. 1927. "Manic-Depressive States and the Pre-Genital Levels of the Libido" in *Selected Papers of Karl Abraham M.D.* London: Hogarth Press.

Allouch, J. 2006. *Erotique du deuil au temps de la mort sèche*. Paris: Distribution Distique Diffusion Stendhal.

Arendt, H. 1968. "Walter Benjamin: 1892–40" in *Men in Dark Times*. New York: Harcourt, 153–206.

Aries, P. 2008. *The Hour of Our Death*. New York: Random House.

Auster, P. 2007. *The Invention of Solitude*. New York: Penguin Books.

Benjamin, W. 1993. *Sonetos*. Barcelona: Ediciones Península.

Benjamin, W. 2011. "Death of the Father" in *Early Writings (1910–1917)*, Cambridge, Massachusetts: The Belknap Press of Harvard University Press, 128–31.

Bermond, D. 1998. "Entrevista a Paul Ricoeur. Afrontar lo imperdonable," *La Nación*, June 24th 1998. https://www.lanacion.com.ar/cultura/afrontar-lo-imperdonable-nid213659/

Borges, J.L. 1971. "An Authobiographical Essay," in *The Aleph and Other Stories*, New York: E. P. Dutton & Co., 135–85.

Díaz Romero, R. 1999. *La pregunta por la técnica del psicoanálisis* [The Question about the Technique of Psychoanalysis]. Rosario: Homo Sapiens

Freud, S. 1953b. "Fragment of an Analysis of a Case of Hysteria" in *SE, Vol. VII.*

Freud, S. 1955a. "Studies on Hysteria" in *SE, Vol. II.*

Freud, S. 1955b. "On Transformations of Instinct as Exemplified in Anal Erotism" in *SE, Vol. XVII*, 125–34.

Freud, S. 1957a. "Mourning and Melancholia" in *SE, Vol. XIV*, 237–58.

Freud, S. 1957b. "On Narcissism" in *SE, Vol. XIV*, 67–104.

Freud, S. 1957c. "On Unconscious" in *SE, Vol. XIV*, 159–215.

Freud, S. 1957d. "Thoughts for the Times on War and Death," in *SE, Vol. XIV*, London: The Hogarth Press, 273–300.

Freud, S. 1958. "Totem and Taboo," in *SE, Vol. XIII*, 1–163.

Freud, S. 1959a. "Inhibitions, Symptoms, and Anguish" in *SE, Vol. XX*, 77–177.

Freud, S. 1961a. "Neurosis and Psychosis" in *SE, Volume XIX*, 149–53.
Freud, S. 1961b. "Some Psychical Consequences of the Anatomical Distinction between the Sexes," *SE, Vol. IXI*. 243–60.
Freud, S. 1961c. "Female Sexuality" in *SE, Vol. XXI*, 223–46.
Freud, S. 1962. "Charcot" in *SE, Vol. III*, 11–23.
Freud, S. 1964. "Analysis Terminable and Interminable" in *SE, Vol. XXIII*, 209–53.
Freud, S. 1966. "Draft G. Melancholia (Undated.? January 7, 1895)" in *SE, Vol. 1*, pp. 200–205.
Freud, S. 1971. "The Interpretation of Dreams." *SE, Vol. IV*.
Grinberg, L. 1992. *Guilt and Depression*. New York: Karnac Books.
Hernández, M. 1985. *Cuaderno del Cancionero y romancero de ausencias,* [Songbook and Balladbook of Absence], Alicante: Instituto de Estudios Juan Gil-Albert.
Hoffmann, E.T.A. 1824. *The Devi's Elixir*. Edinburgh: William Blackwood und London.
Julia, V. 1993. *La tragedia griega* [The Greek Tragedy]. Buenos Aires: Plus Ultra.
Julien, P. 1995. *Le manteau de Noé: essai sur la paternité* [Noah's Mantle] Paris: Desclée de Brouwer.
Kierkegaard, S. 2014. *The Concept of Anxiety*. New York: Liverlight.
Klein, M. 1940. "Mourning and Its Relation to Manic-Depressive States" in *The International Journal of Psycho-Analysis* 21: 125–53.
Klibansky, Panofsky, & Saxl. 1979. *Saturn and Melancholy*. Liechtenstein: Kraus Reprint.
Kovadloff, S. 1996. *Lo irremediable*. Buenos Aires: Ed. Emecé.
Lacan J. 1966. "La place de la psychanalyse dans la médecine [The place of psycho-analysis in medicine]," *Cahier du College de Medicine,* 12: 761–74.
Lacan, J. 1971–1972. *The Seminar of Jacques Lacan: The Knowledge of the Psychoanalyst, 1971–1972*. Unpublished translation by Cormac Gallagher.
Lacan, J. 1978. *The Seminar of Jacques Lacan: The Four Fundamental Concepts of Psychoanalysis: Book XI*. New York: W.W. Norton & Company.
Lacan, J. 1989. "Geneva Lecture on the Symptom," *Analysis No. 1*. Melbourne: Centre for Psychoanalytic Research, 7–26.
Lacan, J. 1997. *The Seminar of Jacques Lacan: The Ethics of Psychoanalysis. Book VII*, New York: Norton & Co.
Lacan, J. 1999. *The Seminar of Jacques Lacan. Book XX: Encore 1972-1973, On Feminine Sexuality, the Limits of Love and Knowledge*. New York: W.W. Norton & Co
Lacan, J. 2006a. "On My Antecedents" in *Écrits: The First Complete Edition in English*. New York: Norton & Co., 51–56.
Lacan, J. 2006b. "Remarks on Daniel Lagache's Presentation: "Psychoanalysis and Personality Structure" in *Écrits: The First Complete Edition in English*. New York: Norton & Co., 543–74.
Lacan, J. 2006c. "The Signification of the Phallus" in *Écrits: The First Complete Edition in English*. New York: W.W. Norton & Co, pp. 575–84.

Lacan, J. 2007. *The Seminar of Jacques Lacan: The Other Side of Psychoanalysis, Vol. Book XVII*, New York: Norton.

Lacan, J. 2014. *Anxiety: The Seminar of Jacques Lacan, Book X.* Cambridge: Polity Press.

Lacan, J. 2018. "Note on the Child" *The Lacanian Review*, no. 4, 13–14.

Lacan, J. 2019a. "The Third," *The Lacanian Review, Get Real*, Issue 07, Spring, 83–112.

Lacan, J. 2019b. *The Seminar of Jacques Lacan: Desire and its Interpretation. Book VI*, Cambridge: Polity.

Lacan, J. 2021. *The Object Relation: The Seminar of Jacques Lacan, Book IV.* Cambridge: Polity.

Lerner, E. 1994. "Ni blanco ni negro II," [Neither Black nor White II] in *Jornadas "20 años de Escuela,"* Buenos Aires: Escuela Freudiana de Buenos Aires, trans. J Campos.

Moliner, M. 2007. *Diccionario de uso del español*, Madrid: Gredos.

Shakespeare, W. 2002. "Sonnet XXII," in *The Oxford Shakespeare: The Complete Sonnets and Poems.* Oxford: Oxford University Press.

Sophocles 2003. *Antigone.* New York: Oxford University Press, trans. by Reginald Gibbons and Charles Segal.

Ulloa, F. 2000. "Sociedad y crueldad," *Página/12*, January 4, 2000.

Vegh, I. 1991. *El melancólico objeto del maldecir* [The Melancholy Object of the Curse] in *Matices* [Nuances]. Buenos Aires: Agalma.

Vidal, E. 1984. "A questão do objeto no campo freudiano" [The Question of the Object in the Freudian Field] in *O objeto na teoria e na prática psicanalítica.* Rio de Janeiro: Ed. Campus.

Glossary

Acting out:

In the *Standard Edition*, Simon Strachey translates the German word *agieren* used by Freud, as acting out. Lacan continues this psychoanalytic tradition using the English word. In Freud's work, the term acting out refers to past events that are not remembered in analysis and return in actions. Lacan develops it further linking it with the dimension of the Other. He underlines the relationship between acting out and the Other. In Seminar X, *Anxiety* (1962–1963), Lacan says, "acting-out is essentially something in the subject's conduct that is on show. The demonstrative aspect of any acting-out, its orientation towards the Other, must be noted" (Lacan 2014, 123).

Agalma:

The literal meaning of this Greek term is a piece of jewelry or precious object. In his discussion of *The Symposium*, Lacan stays that *agalma* is the privileged, hidden, and ungraspable object of desire. Then he conceived the embodiment of *agalma* in the concept of object *a*, the object cause of desire (see Object *a*). In the context of that philosophical dialogue, Lacan says that Socrates is only an envelope of desire, the semblance of object *a*, to whom the question "What do you want?" is addressed.

Holophrasis:

Lacan borrows the concept from linguistics where it designates a single word used as a phrase. He introduces this concept to refer to the clinical manifestations like psychosis, mentally deficient, psycho-somatic illnesses when there is no interval between S1 and S2. That interval is fundamental for the constitution of the subject.

Imaginary, Real, Symbolic:

These three registers (or orders) are the core of Lacan's thought. The Imaginary was the first to appear and was central in his thinking until the mid-1950s. The ego is constituted in the mirror stage by the identification with a unitary image of the body, which is the ground of the imaginary order. From the late 1950s onwards the notion of the "symbolic," as essentially a linguistic dimension, came to the forefront. Following the developments of Saussure and Levi-Strauss, Lacan radicalized them when he says that the subject is himself an effect of the symbolic. The third term "real" stands for what is neither imaginary nor symbolic, lined to the category of the impossible, which is not represented by the image and not mediatized by words. In Seminar XI, *Four Fundamental Concepts of Psychoanalysis* (1964), Lacan defines the real as "the impossible to say," the unsayable.

Melancholia:

Freud delineates the difference between melancholia and mourning since the symptoms of sadness and apathy belong to both. But in melancholia, there is a "loss of the capacity to love, inhibition of all activities, and a lowering of the self-regarding feelings . . . the shadow of the object fell upon the ego" (Freud 1957a, 244–49)

Name-of-the-Father:

In the context of Lacan's three registers, the Name-of-the-Father (*nom-du-père*) refers not to the imaginary father (as a paternal imago), nor the real father, but the symbolic father. The father performs the symbolic function: he names, he gives his name, he transmits the law. According to Lacan, the foreclosure of the Name-of-the-Father is related to the psychosis.

Object *a*:

The symbol *a* is one of the first algebraic signs to appear in Lacan's work. Over years of theorization, Lacan has reformulated it and underlined it. At first, it was called *object petit a.* In the imaginary register, it represents the small other associated with one's own self. Then the term concerns the object cause of desire and the surplus enjoyment (*plus-de-jouir*). The object *a* acquires more and more the connotations of the real. And it performs a fundamental function in Lacanian clinic in which the analyst must position himself as the semblance of object *a*.

Phallus:

Moving away from biological determinism of sexuality Lacan clearly distinguishes Phallus from the penis, and defined it as a signifier. At the beginning of its development, Lacan identifies it as the imaginary phallus, then as "mother's phallus" and finally as "symbolic phallus," which is an empty signifier (an absence). The phallus also plays a role in the sexuation formulas (see Sexuation). *Phallicity* is a derivative noun.

Phantasm:

With his concept, Lacan goes further with Freud's "primal fantasies" (spelled "phantasy" in the *Standard Edition*), which refers to the question of the origins of sexuality. For Lacan, the phantasm is the scene where the subject is located in his impossible encounter with his object of desire. At the same time, the phantasm sustains the desire. *Phantasmatically* is its adverbial form.

Sexuation:

Sexuation defines the speaking being's position in relation to sexuality, the way in which they acquire a sexual position. The Masculine and feminine position is not biological determinism. According to Lacan, sexuation entails a choice, a formal positioning in regards to the phallic function.

Subject:

The notion of the subject has a long history in philosophy, logic, and psychology. Lacan transforms, in the context of Saussure's linguistic theory, the subject of the conscious into the subject of the unconscious. In this way, he underlines the function of desire for the subject. The term *Subjectivating* is a derivation of subject. It refers to the process that allows the speaking being, through the times of mourning, to release from the ties to the lost object and accede to a position of desire.

Sublimation:

In 1905, Freud develops the concept of sublimation to give an account of the particular human activities like artistic or intellectual which appear to have no connection with sexuality jet are channeled by sexual drives. The products of sublimation are always socially and highly estimated.

Supplement:

The English term "supplement" generally refers to something that is added to something else to improve. In psychoanalysis concerns a substitute for what is missing at the level of the symbolic and impels the subject to carry out something extra.

Index

About the Author

Adriana Bauab is psychoanalyst, vice president of the Freudian School of Buenos Aires and exdirector and professor of the postgraduate course in psychoanalysis at the Centro de Salud Mental N° 3 "Dr. Ameghino." She has published in many national and international reviews. Other of her books—*De la angustia al deseo* and *El psicoanálisis en la escena contemporánea.* She develops her clinical practice in Buenos Aires city (Argentina).

www.ingramcontent.com/pod-product-compliance
Ingram Content Group UK Ltd.
Pitfield, Milton Keynes, MK11 3LW, UK
UKHW041843031026
15587UKWH00002B/979

9 781793 617750